A bundle of cultureshocking news

Created by: Jiu Ling © 2015
Cover by: Jiu Ling
Back by: Jiu Ling, based on a scene by Terry Richardson
Pictures by: Jiu Ling, except "Futurama Fry"

Published by Global Citizen ePub, available on Amazon, Kobo & Google Play

50 SHADES OF CHINA (5$ digital bundle)

Kobo/Google ISBN 978-3-95694-004-0
Amazon ISBN 978-3-95694-005-7

CHINA BEST BEHAVED COUNTRY (3$ stand alone)

Kobo/Google ISBN 978-3-95694-006-4
Amazon ISBN 978-3-95694-007-1

CHINA MOST MISBEHAVED COUNTRY (3$ stand alone)

Kobo/Google ISBN 978-3-95694-008-8
Amazon ISBN 978-3-95694-009-5

Dedication

To Mao, her family&students.

I want you to become well acquainted, on first name terms if you will, with my favorite and most cherished China...

- <u>A note to the 50 Shades...-Fanatic</u>

I hope the semi-quote didn't stir your hunger for a spiced-up "Dream of the Red Chamber". I'm sorry if this isn't quite the next steamy Twilight-fanfic some of you were looking for (although many books on Chinese etiquette cross the border to fiction). If I can still manage to hold those fans of 50 Shades, here you'll get to know the rubber-band relationship with Chinese etiquette – highly enticing, sometimes teasing, always passionate.

This package bundles the two guides CHINA BEST BEHAVED COUNTRY and CHINA MOST MISBEHAVED COUNTRY. With those two titles at hand, I'm counting on you to be a fan of the paradox and the superlative (that always helps when dealing with China). Get ready for some comedy as well, since this is a case of serious infotainment with China on first name terms. I know, writing comedy about cultures is wrong, but holy hell is it fun.

For the reader who likes:
- the intercultural challenge
- a business/work/travel/politics or study mission to succeed
- awesome first-hand anecdotes
- vivid metaphors
- a fun read

And for those who fancy the bundle, here I am, boasting not only one book on Chinese etiquette. Two of them they are. My cow!

The first book is for home salon study - outside China, still in the comfort zone - while the second one caters to the expat and China alumni. It's full of charming details that will strike a chord in many of you. Both volumes are suited for the noob all the way to the expert. Though they are labeled as guides, they're not supposed to steer you. Exploit them in your fashion and apply your legit lot or little of background knowledge. And "Jeez!": don't worry too much about theory. Put it right into practice!

- ## A note to the guru and their critics

Putting things into practice... Fair enough, but some of us care about theory, right? All you guys and gals, working as intercultural trainers, facilitators and researchers, you deserve a lot more impact on society. I hope my books can help you. Comparing the BEST to the MOST will offer you some new and exciting insight. The bundle, in particular, can shed a new light on how to convey acting competence in any intercultural endeavor. People might mouth off those "gurus" who're only "selling useful advice". Well in that case, the 50 Shades-approach will prove them wrong. You can create those thought-provoking seminars that shape personalities and may this here provide you an engaging read.

Untangle the fuss - for the sake of your trainees! Equip yourself with strong and convincing explanations for concepts that used to be too complex. As an input, I'm offering my own way of looking at culture and etiquette. What I do is using metaphors: vivid images, painted in words.

• A note to germophobics and scholars

When you read Book 1 CHINA BEST BEHAVED COUNTRY you will think I'm obsessed with nature, metaphorizing DNA and germs and what else.

To give you an example, let me recall that beautiful summer when I attended a guru camp on the topic of intercultural competence. In a discussion on concepts, I came up with my way of understanding "culture": "To me, culture is the dark and moist corner of my fridge. Like a colony of mildew that multiplies and develops through exchange." I stopped right there for the crowd. In the world of metaphors, there's always a place to stop for the crowd. In my head, however, I followed the thread. I imagined how the rest of my fridge would be full of microscopic bits of culture. I saw bio-cultures traveling through the fridge and teaming up with others, creating something totally new: the "intercultural". Just like every culture of mildew, the intercultural is boundless. In a way, the intercultural is a culture by itself. If that applies, every culture is intercultural, too. In other words: We're all just social germs traveling through a very big fridge.

- ## A note to Mum

Alright, Mum, I swear: My fridge isn't brimming with rotten biology! Don't worry too much about my flat. Besides that, I'm still thinking of a metaphor that has a better connotation than mildew. For now, let us see it as a painting in words. I'm sure some of the writers among you will find them a case of writer's fail. Don't hold it against me. Take it as my last attempt to keep those 50 Shades-fans ;-) ! In any case, the 50 shades from the title are a little exaggerated. If I claim to paint China (and I think that's mostly the case in Book 1) I'm painting it in 7 shades only. 7 fundamentals of Chinese BEST behavior. Book 1 gives China a face, a body and a brain. Book 2 adds the humor and the heart. Sometimes the heart doesn't do what the brain wants and the other way around (It's the same with us people, isn't it?). Don't be disappointed if Book 2 will jeopardize the wisdom of Book 1 – I told you to equip for the paradox.

CHINA MOST MISBEHAVED COUNTRY goes pop and punk with stereotypes, images and the fear of using them both. It offers you even more concrete scenarios in colorful anecdotes. Enjoy!

- <u>A final note to the guru and their clients:</u>

You're going to realize that I'm writing with and against many of the trainings' conventions. That's because I endorse the profession of an intercultural trainer. I want those clients to flock to your seminars, thus make them be good. Don't sell the promise of a shortcut. When dealing with China, there's no shortcut anyway. And there're no promises, either. China will always surprise the trainee - and the trainer as well! Most of us will agree on the following: if you can choose between Culture for Dummies and a tough but enlightening journey, opt for the latter. As a Chinese saying goes: "The journey is the reward." And yes, China can be tough. A journey without GPS. Google Maps might get you to Starbucks, but it won't get you to succeed in your business/travel/politics mission.

Sending you and your clients on a journey with this, I'll let you construct etiquette. Joyfully and shamelessly! I'm sure you will add your reflections and experience to make this trip unique. Ultimately, you will come to the point where you start to destruct. And it will be rewarding, I promise. An engaging way of dealing with culture helps you more than any theory. Please leave a review to share your experience!

And, of course, keep exchanging. As always.

Jiu Ling's CHINA BEST BEHAVED COUNTRY

Prologue

I'm sure you want to know what's Chinese BEST behavior. From why I put that word in capitals to everything else. Since I pulled that typographic stunt, I can't blame you for asking me to kindly lift the curtain, thin out the fog and kill the magic. To be honest, Chinese BEST behavior remains a mystery to me in a number of ways. And yet in the logic of BEST, I offer myself to work as your guide in a maze.

If I was to imagine my maze-running fellows, I'd draw you in your prettiest feature: the many question marks looming above your head. This book was made by all the great questions I've been asked about Chinese etiquette. It's for everyone who can't stop asking and won't stop asking, even after this book. I'll present you my best-of China conversations in the shape of so-called memes. A meme? That's a talking picture, like the one below:

HANG ON...

I THINK I'VE SEEN THIS BEFORE

All memes were created using MemeGenerator (an app by Alberto Garcia Hierro). They're based on my own photographs, except the one above of course. I hope you can go with that.

(PRAIRIE KID:) NEVER MIND, I GUESS NO ONE'S WATCHIN'

Well then...

...SO WHAT ABOUT THIS BEST?

TELL ME MORE ABOUT IT!

BEST is about putting things in practice, about reflection and dialogue. Besides sharing my knowledge and experience, I will lay out a few paths of thought to explore. It's up to you to walk them and observe what it does to you. You can discuss the topics with your friends and family, even if they haven't been to China before. You can re-read this book after a trip to the country. It will make you see its content in a different light and the dialogue in *you* will proceed. This being said, the journey you'll take is not a walk in the park.

Chinese BEST behavior

A maze

Sometimes, navigating Chinese etiquette is like running through a maze that constantly changes its shape and comes up with new traps and pitfalls. The floor you just treaded on is crumbling, the walls along the corridor you chose are closing in. A false step can trigger an avalanche. But it won't, because you learn. You grow and develop the skills to handle the hardships, surprises and traps. You discover some secret doors, and eventually, you even overcome the greatest obstacle of the intercultural maze: getting lost in a state of confusion.

Instead, you accept the way this labyrinth works. That the deeper you delve, it challenges more, reveals more and teaches you more. Most of all, you accept that you'll never get out of it. Though that, of course, is a later stage in the process.

In this book, we're not getting there, not even close. I can't let you leap the stages of learning, of taking in certain facts about China before I'll ask you to unlearn them. For now, I will herd you through the basics of Chinese mentality, which includes a bit of history, philosophy, common Chinese concepts and a handful of practical explanations outside the "history, Laozi, Buddha and Confucius"-mantra.

<u>The social context: the sparkling fella on the loo</u>

METAPHOR ALERT

What do you get when morning dew sneezes at a spider's web?

Exactly, the China sparkle. You see it glistening in the morning light? That's the one I'm talking about. Each string of the cobweb is a thread in the game of Chinese connex. Every little dew'ldy droplet is a germ of Chinese mentality. When a group of BEST behaved Chinese meet, it's an epidemic of sparkle, like someone plucks a string and the little droplets spray all over the net, mix, divide and bounce. And with every BEST act, they dance and dance and dance… (metaphor fade-out)

Chinese BEST behavior shows only in a social setting. This is why I chose the image of a cobweb. I want you to see it, to spot the sparkle and look at the context of behaviour. Chinese people act in the context of their family relations, friendships and business ties. This doesn't mean they only sparkle among folks, friends, bosses and colleagues. Even a fella who is squattingly squatting a toilet (the most private place there is), puffing his cigarette, reading the paper, picking his nose and ignoring the queue in front of his privy: he's not acting outside the China context. A context, in which people surround him all day. For once he has found a place for his own, and now, they're slamming at his door. Mercilessly, they're pestering him with their own little urgencies. "They", in fact, classify as "Chinese strangers" on his network-map. The fella will take his time, sparkling ever so gently. Even the anti-social takes place within the social.

Loo or no loo, germs on a spider's trap isn't the most charming picture Mother Nature has in stock. Then again, who hasn't marveled at the beauty of a cobweb glistening in morning dew? The China sparkle is equally fascinating. It's the friendly host and the selfish fella, the curious restaurant owner and the shrewd business partner. We will get back to the networks in a chapter or two, without the cobweb, I promise. Next, I'm going to explain why Chinese people sparkle from inside.

Explaining Chinese BEST behavior: mental DNA

No, it's not for the capital letters, and I don't think that Chinese people have a certain DNA that sets them straight in all the ways this horrible wording implies. "Mental DNA" is simply more elegant. I could also be very down to earth and call it "meat and potatoes", saying what it is: the core components of Chinese mentality, which I pinpoint to history and philosophy - and to add some flavor, social negotiation.

If history and philosophy are the meat and potatoes, "Social Negotiation" is the secret ingredient I stole from the Haute Cuisine of Social Sciences. The sensation of this spice is intriguing, but let's not sprinkle it on the empty plate. Since it's me who's dishing up, I might as well share my recipe with you:

I will touch upon history and philosophy in the first chapters of this book. In the second half, I'll strip the big term "social negotiation" off its fancy sciences dress, showing how a DNA app would make the Internet collapse. In this recipe, all the steps follow in a certain order (Background briefing >> Examples >> Reflection). On the larger scale of your China agenda, I recommend you to do the same, scheduling a peek into history/philosophy first.

China's history and philosophy are ideal subjects for the rocking chair explorer who doesn't leave the fireplace. Get some books at the public library nearby, since what I pack in here can only scrape the surface. Later, when in China, visit museums and monuments, stay at people's homes, attend festivals, watch parades, roam in bookstores and tour sites until you're all templed up. In combination, cozy home study and travel work best.

How to turn a boring exhibition into a book full of wonder: A Xi'An example

The Steele Forest in Xi'An doesn't compare to the nearby Mount Hua or the Terracotta Warriors in terms of, well, anything. However, it's a good spot to escape the crowds and reflect on China. I see it as one of the most underrated tourist sites in Xi'An. Many other visitors would call it a garden stroll with a ticket price. Roaming the place full of rocks and trees, they were flicking through quotes by Confucius. Despite the translations, the guy would remain an enigma to most.

Personally, I didn't have this feeling when I read-walked the Stone Steele Forest. It was my background knowledge that turned this exhibition into something engaging. Even that little knowledge made me see the quotes carved in stone in a different light. Here's my "how to turn a boring exhibition into a book full of wonder"-Confucius-example:

1st: Expose yourself to that spark of inspiration. Read some Confucian quotes.

2nd: Web search Confucianism and how it seeped into the workings of an empire. Combine history and philosophy.

3rd: Marvel at the script stele forest in Xi'An, a display of Confucian quotes carved in stone.

China doesn't start at the airport. It will invite you to learn from it and deal with it, no matter where you are. It's up to you to accept this invitation. Sure, not all of us can spare the evening hour for a quiet round of reading. Or fair enough, they prefer to spend their free time with more exciting things than dynasties and Dao. The key: Whatever has you reflecting on China makes your mission succeed. It's not about the amplitude of your scholarly ambitions. It's about the dialogue within.

I cherish my Chinese cornerstones. This is why I've always embraced the idea of a "mental DNA", all the way throughout the making of my dialogue. My China journey has led me past various stages: the fireplace, the open field, the learning, disappointment, confusion and the stage of un-learning. Even now that I've come to having fun with it a lot*, China wouldn't work for me without those precious cornerstones (*for proof see my second book, CHINA MOST MISBEHAVED COUNTRY).

The draw-by-numbers method

Precious, precious cornerstones. Let us find yours, doing it like drawing-by-numbers. In this book, we're drawing China by numbers, but unlike the complex shapes from our early learners drawing book, we're operating on 7 steps only. Once we got the general outline, I'll let you make it your own work of art. You will tweak out the details, get a perspective on things and trace the fine line of China's dos and don'ts. And even after that, things won't be done and dusted.

Drawing China is a never-ending process and the 50 Shades-approach will be your long-term companion. As you develop a feel for the BEST, you willingly discard the straight line between 1 and 2, adding a fine number of bends. The showy curves and ornamental shapes from 111 to 407 will appear as pompous explanations. You blow out the fuss and give it a clear cut instead. You accept that your very own China has its clumsy sides, parts that not even you, who created this thing, may get a grip on for now. You accept that your China has edges.

Number 1: backgrounds

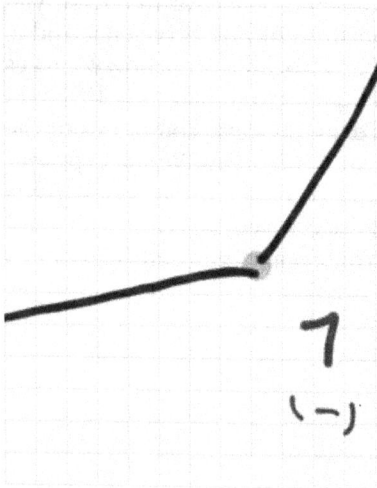

I base this book on one single claim.
(Spotlight, drum rolls, encroachment of artificial fog)
That China cannot but be the BEST BEHAVED COUNTRY in the world.
Why?

Because every action happens in front of a background, and in China the act and the stage make a thrilling combination. They turn Chinese BEST behavior into an often hilarious, always particular and sometimes puzzling-yet-charming play. The actors and the stage - China and its people - are fascinating and likable, we can't deny that. But on the flip side of backgrounds, Chinese families, peers and society tend to define roles for their folks. That's the case like in any other country.

BUT WHAT HAPPENED

TO CHINESE CONFORMISM???

In China, messing with the script is on the rise. It's up to every individual to act within the confines of expectations or not. So-called rebellions happen in the same place, in front of the same background as the norm. Even misbehaviour is a type of behaviour. If we follow that thought, behavior can be anything, right? Be it a habit, a general courtesy, a rite or simply the action of not reacting at all. Nowadays, people find their ways to queerstep the norm. Lifestyles, careers and looks are constantly changing, the Chinese claim their freedom to choose. Their choices may inflict a change in China. More often though, their choices actually *reflect* the change. It's not even a paradox: The backgrounds have evolved, but they hold their ground as an influence on Chinese BEST behavior.

Climate, food, laws, borders, norms and connotations, they're all background. Our living spheres become tattoos on our body and mind. They make us see the world through our own pair of glasses. They create a reality exclusively linked to culture. My reality might differ from yours, because my values and traditions are different.

Now imagine you meet someone from Hell's Kitchen, New York City. Would you prefer to talk and interact or simply read what it says on his back, provided he's got "Hell's Kitchen made me" inked all across? Personally, I'd prefer to interact. Even if the tattoo might out him as a true Kitchen breed, it doesn't really credit much else. A tattoo may prove you some street cred. In the same manner, all our backgrounds could be nothing but street cred. A box full of hashtags. Stereotypes. That's why we need to look beyond the tattoo. Every action is interaction. It refers to our roots, either by showing or concealing them.

Hell's Kitchen
China
Wherever

Growing up in your setting(s) gives you a mental DNA. Not only conformity, also acts of rebellion highlight your roots. Especially when it shows what you rebel against. It's no big science to recognize the backdrop of norms and conventions that always tried to mold you. While it doesn't always surface as an influence, China's history of thought is the most prominent background.

Number 2: history of thought

On a topographic map of China's leaders and thinkers, we'd surely have Mao Zedong, Deng Xiaoping and Sun Yatsen crowning the landscape. You can't deny their influence on modern China's mental state, but don't forget the underlying life support. Next to the peaks, there's the country's network of subterranean runnels. Albeit invisible, they're a major part of the landscape, nourishing the ground. This system of water vessels is the BEST-of ancient Chinese thought: Daoism, Confucianism and Buddhism.

(SHANGHAI SUBURBIAN FORUM TROLL:)

EXACTLY. SO WHAT WE HAD HERE WAS A WHOLE TREASURE BOX OF CULTURAL HERITAGE. AND THEN CAME MAO! AND WHAT HE DID WAS, WITH HIS CULTURAL REVOLUTION, HE ERADICATED WHAT HAD BEEN THERE FOR MILLENIA! GONE! FOREVER!

Well... not quite. To tell you the truth, the damage wasn't deep enough to last. Not even the Cultural Revolution could uproot this meat of a potato. The movement lasted from 1966 to 1976 and spanned across every social and cultural sphere. Besides trying other things, the boil was aimed at ancient and religious customs. After Mao's death, it was an awkward revelation that even the Chairman's revolution couldn't change the nation's DNA. Confucian principles are engrafted in politics, education and public discourse. Like script carved in stone.

When Chinese people talk about food they often end up discussing Yin and Yang and the Five Elements – common knowledge that derives from the Dao. Discussing food, health and healthy food, Chinese people can talk the night. Buddhism plays a role in everyday lives, in little personal rituals, family customs and in the advent of big exams or major business missions – when people tend to pray.

> *Does the population divide into something like confessions?*

I wouldn't say so. Only few will refer to themselves as "a Daoist" or say something like "I am a Buddhist and I don't believe in Confucianism". There are differences between the three lines of thought, but they never managed to tear society apart. "I am a Daoist and I pray to Buddhist gods and believe in Kong Zi's words." That is what you're going to hear. By means of compromise, China's big old three (Confucianism, Daoism and Buddhism) have managed to form a BEST of Chinese thought.

San Jiao Fa Yi

Under the banner of "San Jiao Fa Yi" Chinese believers all become one. The words mean "Three religions, making one". However, compromise is more than just a blackbox of temples, Goddess donations and aphorisms. It exceeds the religious domain.

Number 3: compromise

METAPHOR ALERT

Imagine a factory that produces BEST behaviour. There'd be the rule-of-law compartment, the authority wing and some other divisions that all produce BEST behaviour. Asking you in Chinese terms: Which division would become model department of the work unit? - It would be the faculty of "Chinese ancient thought", because it's a teamwork-of-three, joining forces at the assembly line for compromise. It's a shared principle in Confucianism, Daoism and Buddhism.

In their BEST behavior, Chinese people seem to be ever-resourceful in reaching a compromise - like it was really for the title "model worker of the unit of the month". I regularly marvel at how the Chinese seem to arch their backs. (And I'm not talking about Chinese acrobatics!)

I often wonder if it's hard to manage all these balancing acts; if the compromise is an agreement or maybe just a sop; if they finish negotiations with a frown or a warm feeling in their chest, the one that jingles "Mission accomplished!".

And often, to be honest, I can't really tell.

The birth pangs connected to compromise are a silent phenomenon: In a conflict, many Chinese people will try their BEST to avert an escalation. Pulling a classy compromise, they won't name their concessions (as in "For the record, I let you..."). Their polite give-and-take may leave you with little in terms of interpretation.

In the event of clashing interests you won't get a tsunami of curses and rage. Instead, you'll get a shallow and silent, unfathomable lake. You ask yourself: "So what happened? What exactly has been compromised?"

I can only give an un-answering answer: Yes. It's an art to compromise and make it seem so effortless.

I'm speaking of a people with some very BEST skill. But what about the Average Ma? How does the individual feel about family-friendship-and-business ties that can, at times, appear to you like shackles?

Some of them handle conflicts with ease, others let you notice it's a bugger, but they go through it the same. Some appear plausible in all of their actions, others are perplexing. In the end, they leave you with no clue for a judgement of events. I wish I could introduce a harmony-tracker-of-sorts, one that lets you debrief a conflict, but I'm afraid, there seems to be no app for that! (I will talk about another killer-app in our final Number 7.) The only advice I can give is

To all who'll go to China very soon, here's a clever trick to gather some useful material: Stay away from the good-foreign-visitor game. Pull an epic Laowai for at least a couple of days, provided you have time to switch back to blending in when you're done. In those Epic Laowai-Days, there's only one advice: don't follow, don't imitate, don't assimilate at all. Act the most foreign to them as you can (you've probably done that without wanting it) and the fantastic world of Chinese-foreign relations will unfold in front of your eyes.

HANG ON... OH, NO NO NO NO!

THOSE FOREIGNERS ARE WAY TOO AWKWARD!

Their behaviour towards foreigners is a complex matter, but still of course an instance of BEST: Chinese people seem to oscillate between two extremes. There's the welcoming face, namely curiosity, friendliness, hospitality and even fandom frenzy. Beijing Huanying Ni! That's one face of the BEST. Then there is the different BEST, the one that leaves you feeling excluded, feeling "othered" by endless remarks of your foreignness. While they'd certainly pounce at you for English practice, you can be sure to scare them away by asking for directions. Others might eye you and "hellou!" you, many will smile at you a smile that could mean a million things. Sometimes, when you hit the street, you sense a shift in their squatting position, you sense it as a response to your presence in their neighborhood, in their town, their province, their country... Every wall you project in their minds will pop up within you as well. Every beam of spotlight will make you feel like it's all about you.

"It's me! It's me, it's me, it's me!" Even if you put it in more eloquent words, the feeling you express would still be the same and I can't really blame you for that.

Chinese do make a difference between foreigners and themselves. To them, you're like a creature that has come through a hole in the sky. While they single out workmates, friends and family from the whole population, the way they treat you differently is even more special.

What is the difference between foreigners being foreign and a stranger slamming at a locked bathroom door?

As you already know, the fella on the loo acts within context. The way he treats those queuing strangers is selfish, but understandable. Everyone involved can place it in a shelf with a label - they can spot each other on the map. If there was his mother, boss or buddy in queue, he'd probably get his skates on his business.

Now... the thing with you is: People can't place you in a network and thereby come in shades at you. The background is theirs, not yours. This is a crucial observation (and also the reason why I recommend a time in which you act as foreign as possible). It will help you accept their fuzziness. Just try to see them in front of their background, and then try to see yourself the way *they* do.

(WISDOM DEER:)
HENCE,

MY USEFUL CONCEPT OF
'BACKGROUND' ALSO
GUIDES.... THEM?

Exactly, but probably not as much in their dealings
with you. Is it a luck or a pity? A little bit of both, I
guess.

What follows is a collection of background
influences, the magic that steers the Chinese
people.

Background "ren tai duo"

Chinese drivers cutting lanes, travellers cutting ticket booth queues. They're sick of each other! "Ren tai duo" – There are too many people - is a common phrase in China.

Unlike fellow-Chinese, you are never too much. You're new, you're special, you're strange. Hence, there is room for development on the Chinese-to-foreigners domain. Attitudes towards foreigners have been changing. There are more and more "Laowai" in China, but not enough to make you blend in perfectly.

Background "century of humiliation"

Hostility towards foreigners is almost-not-heard-of... but only almost. Those cases are rare, they happen in front of a historic background and they never target a foreigner as an individual. Many historians pinpoint animosities to a collective feeling of remorse. During a century of humiliation (1840-1940) China was partly colonised by the West and occupied by Japan. It goes without saying that national history is a great source of collective memory. Gladly, more and more Chinese people make their own, un-collective experiences, creating a better future with their foreign friends.

Background "world map"

Shades of envy are just as rare as outward hostility. After the century of humiliation, China saw the West on the rise, but itself didn't start to glitz'n'glam it till the '90s. Since then, development has kicked in full gear. China is prospering. We get to recognise it as a superpower. Envy's slowly ceding for pride. If they pay attention to it, foreign visitors can feel that.

Sure, all these things are merely ego matters and mostly linked to money and power. And still, we shouldn't snoot them: They are the reason why loosing face is sometimes more critical with foreigners around. In a bizarre way, we all carry a mental world map with and within us, and there's a time in our lives when we even embrace those maps as a cute little toy. The "Big-Ego-World-Map". We use it to make comparisons, abuse it to grow an ego, until we shred the ego and fold the map back in. Sooner or later, we grow out of that toy. In comparison, the network plan of Chinese connex is a way more useful kind of map.

(GOLD MAN:)
SO THERE'S ACTUALLY A MAP OF SOCIAL COBWEBS? GURRRRRAIIIIT!!!

The map of social cobwebs is an imaginary one, nested in the workings of each fella's mind. It shows family circles, friends, workmates, strangers, but also goes deeper than that. It makes a big brother act like a big brother and not like a younger brother. It makes an employee an employee, not a boss. In a way, it's their guide to good behaviour with others. Others... but you! You could be a friend-and-foe, boss-and-slave, saviour-invader. Thus I don't call them with you "good". I call them BEST.

Foreigners are met with open-mindedness, respect and admiration. They are met with shyness, suspicion and uncertainty, too. The more you accept your own ambiguities, your own 50 shades, the more you accept them in their contradicting attitudes and policies.

I know you want to join the circle. I know you're longing for a spot on their map, but try to see it from a positive note: The map of social networks comes with sticky obligations. Chinese people have to keep track of their complicated favour-trading-routes. In their mesh of peers, they have to act in pre-defined roles. There is less room to punk it among folks.

In China, families are big and sometimes suffocating. As a Zhong Guo Ren, your compatriots are everywhere, they all speak your language and you cannot simply vent off in public. Meeting a foreigner can be a welcome escape from the rulings of the map.

Chinese people usually embrace the potential that comes with the unknown creature that fell out a hole in the sky. To them, it's a BEST way of learning and (if they dare to go beyond the cliché) un-learning. For you, it's a BEST way to understand the art of compromise.

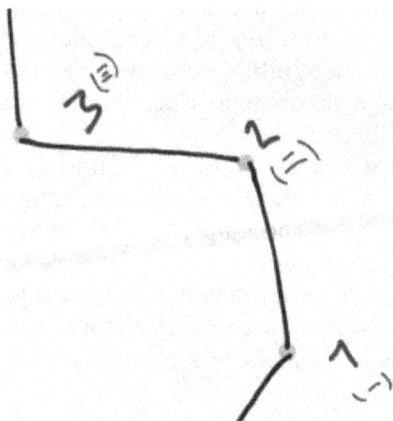

Having come this far, let's have a look at our drawing-by-numbers. We went from backgrounds to compromise, taking the route via history. Backgrounds define our mental DNA, they influence our actions and attitudes. China's history of thought provides a rich source of reference points for daily life ethics and religion. "San Jiao Fa Yi" (Three religions, make one) gives us a first glance on the meaning of compromise. We can see this muscle in action, mostly in the art of conflict management. By the same token, there's a hot pot of attitudes towards foreigners. The sour ones rarely bubble up. The majority of Chinese people will greet you warm-heartedly.

Number 4: talks, trust and timing

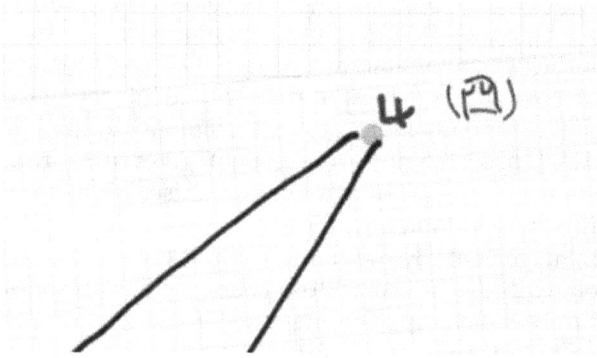

We're about to reach the midway point on our drawing, going from 3 to 4. Let's give ourselves a pat on the back.

Time to make a confession to my readers. As an author, I vow to be honest with whoever you are. As I hope you come from many walks of life, I should speak to all of you.

So here's to honesty. There's actually a spot for you

on the map. I lied about that. I did it on purpose, for the sake of timing. How else could I have mentioned the burden that comes with a spot on the map? I painted the cobweb like there's never been a spider, I cushioned you into an oh-so-cozy observer mode, spared you from social obligations, and I even let you be as foreign as you possibly could. Knowing there's no wild card for anyone, I cheated myself into believing that most of my readers will be grandmas. You know, the ones who want to make a good impression when they finally meet their granddaughter's Chinese fiancé. Sure, extended family dinners can spark an intercultural dialogue and I'd love to have a granny reader. Her intention to build dear bonds with a new family member would shine, but seriously:

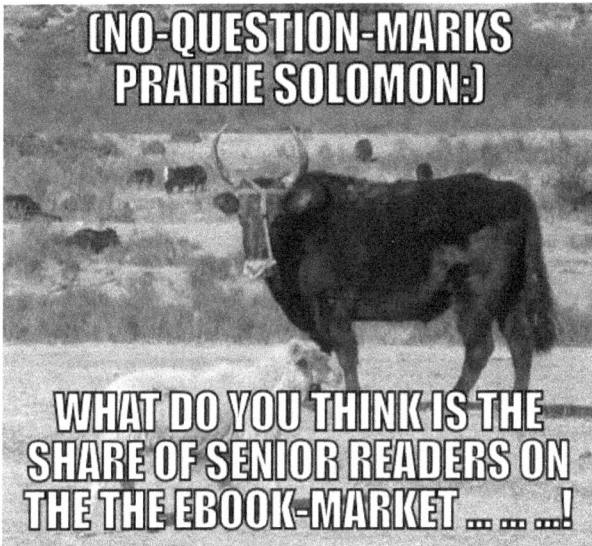

(NO-QUESTION-MARKS PRAIRIE SOLOMON:)

WHAT DO YOU THINK IS THE SHARE OF SENIOR READERS ON THE THE EBOOK-MARKET ... ...!

Waking up on this, I had to aim way beyond the Silver Generation. If I wanted to include the most important facts, I had to consider the Laowai VIP: people in trade, in politics, in business and in cultural exchange. Since the next chapters will be more about communication, I should boost your Talks, Trust and Timing. This formula should echo in your gains. Students of Business Relations will be familiar with the 3 T's, but no matter who you are, Chinese etiquette will prime your pump. On grounds of the 3-T-formula, I will often think of you as a businessperson, just to provide you with examples in a context. It goes without saying that the advice helps all readers the same.

An islet of certainty

On today's global stage, business ways are converging towards a world-wide standard, even though so far, it mostly shows in dress codes and other minor details. Not much of a common ground, but an islet of certainty at least. Probably enough to get you seated around a dinner table in China, which, by the way, is a BEST setup for business deals.

It's likely that people who dine with you will also feed you. They'll put chops and chunks on your plate. That's probably not part of your islet of certainty, but it means you're on the map of social networks - maybe not in the centre, but somewhere in the business corner. It's the little common ground which has brought you here, and with that savory gift on your plate you vaguely sense it:

Beyond that islet, there's a vast territory - The Big
Unknown.

(LITTLE HOOD-
RUNAWAYS:)

HAO DE. LET'S HIT THE
WILD BLUE YONDER.

<u>Dinner talk pitfalls</u>

You can have a nice dinner conversation until you cross to politics. Sure, you came to China with more than a wallet and a belly. You bring your own opinions, fair enough. But what if you also brought a Trojan horse, unknowingly, in the shape of your media preferences (left, right, radical, moderate, mainstream, indie, Chinese and Western). Once the talk on politics crosses borders, it becomes charged with media opinions. Furthermore, there's this musk scent of a big-ego-world-map in the air. Remind yourself, you've grown out of that!

Dangerously, they'd love to discuss Chinese politics at length with you. Usually, they know that most politically-minded foreign visitors are disappointed by China – either because the country's not "left" enough or not "open" enough. Harmlessly, most visitors are not politically minded. You know who you are, but who are they? The Average Ma will keep their politics in place, meaning they discuss it with family and friends, neighbors and workmates. Only those who identify as "public enemies of China" will pull you at your sleeve to the playground of bashing. Expect them to unfold the complete list of 99 problems in China.

Last but not least, there's the citizen type, who addresses certain issues like freedom of the press and labour conditions. "Does that go in the dissident slot?" - Be careful. Don't pull out the whole list yourself, unless you're 100% sure who you're talking to. What if they're not dissidents, but nationalists? Chinese nationalists fiercely discuss politics and even criticise, but only for the better of their motherland. They can compromise their fanatic China-love with their knowledge of the country's issues. That's why they put you in BEST danger to make a fool of yourself.

<u>Deal-breakers</u>

You'll probably need a shot of rice wine to digest the various savory dishes and topics of a Chinese dinner night. Once there's rice wine, things are nearing the climax – the deal.
Business as usual, there will be power struggles, conflicting interests and bargain schemes, but try not to play an ultimatum. That would seem like pressing a gun at someone's chest, pushing their backs against the wall. Instead, aim for the compromise, know that there is something closer-to-BEST for all of you. Next you get a list of deal

breakers in Chinese business talk.

Asking a big Yes/No-question.

(POINTING-AT-ROOSTER-THIEF DUDE:)

HANG ON! DID YOU STEAL THE ROOSTER?

Is it? Will you? Did he? Really? The big Yes/No-questions. Like the ones that show on the strained hero's face, right before the cliff-hanger moment. Then it's a week till the next episode. In real life, however, ain't nobody got time for a week between question and answer. Real life isn't a TV-drama. The more your question electrifies the atmosphere like a Hollywood showdown, the worse for your negotiations.

Chinese don't do glossy Hollywood, they sparkle. Yes/No-questions are a possible dead-end. If it's not A then it's B, and one of them sounds like a fork on a blackboard. Ultimately, this sound will echo in the realms of "face and grace". Yes/No-questions deprive your partner of any chance to wrap a negative response in some nice-sounding words. They elicit an in-your-face-"No!". Even if "No!" is the essence of the news...

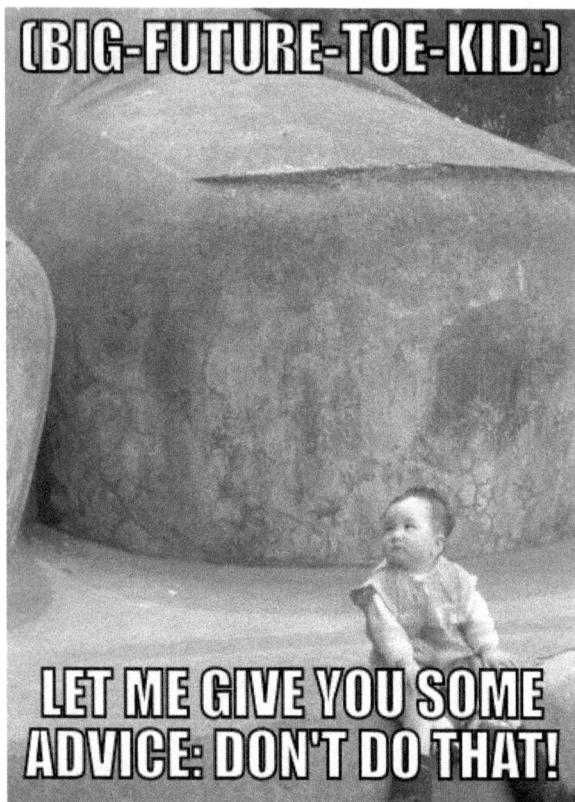

Bad news is like a cart full of poo on top of a hill. You can either push it down the steep end, where it rushes down the slope, reaches maximum speed and hits the target efficiently (quickly & hard).
You can also let the cart take on a trail via flowery landscapes. After the detour, the cart will have slowed down to a degree that when it reaches the target, it only nudges it gently. That's the BEST way to deliver a cartful.

Criticism

Apply a similar attitude when you criticise someone. Wrap it in generous praise. Don't talk about correcting a mistake, talk about improvements. As a leader, don't tell your team to get out of that mess. Call out a turn for the better. Don't ask for excuses and embarrassing explanations, ask for suggestions.

(THE "WE"-FANATIC:)

LET'S BE SERIOUS ABOUT
BECOMING THE BEST!

This is the stuff they will recognize from company keynote-speeches, school gatherings and televised propaganda. Maybe it surprises you, but this kind of stuff works like fire & gasoline. To most expatriates, China is an over-energetic country. I guess it's because people don't drag each other down.

Yet in management, there are times when you have to hit the brakes. Imagine your factory supplier heading for a castle in the sky, floating on some untrue claims that simply suit their vision. You have to tell them what they say isn't true, that actually, it's a dreamy lot of drivel. And you know better than to rub it in their face. To your Chinese counterpart "not true" translates BEST into "false" and "worthless", tags that leave an imprint on that person's reputation. Simple advice: Bite your tongue on those harmful words. Let the facts do the talking, for example, point at sales figures that enlighten the issue. In this way, your business partner may take the lesson without taking the blow.

(THUMBS-UP-JIMI:)

ACT AS IF YOU WERE A
WRITER OF FICTION,
IT HELPS!

In journalism and writing, we are taught "Show don't tell". It means that when your main character feels fear, describe her feeling in detail. Let the reader be with her by means of her senses, her agitated speech or a filter of impressions. By contrast, 'she's in fear' would classify as telling. In Chinese palaver, telling is the steep mountain slope with the cart rushing down. Showing is the slow-trail alternative. Just like those figures for our factory partner. Our intention was to strip them off their phony weapons they've been using in the argument. Making our own point, we can braid in some evidence to prove them wrong. We can convey the truth without the screech of a fork on the blackboard. The famous goose bumps in a novel are the diagram in China's BEST business etiquette.

Summing up, our fine little spot on the map comes with great responsibilities. At times, unleashing blame or dissent feels like we're handling a cart full of poo on top of a hill. Adapt to the rhythm and pace of Chinese BEST behavior. Express your thoughts in a way that communicates implicitly. "Show don't tell" lets you write your story of success. Speaking of that, we don't even have to take a leap to arrive at our next destination: Chinese fantasy language.

Number 5: Chinese fantasy language

As you've probably noticed there are endless ways of beating around the bush, tackling the conflict, pushing the cart and pointing the finger. The Chinese have their ways to share their discontent, and yes, there are metaphorical flames raging inside their metaphorical chests. A vague expression can be charged with strong opinions and feelings. We have to learn to read them. The following phrases show-don't-tell what's going on in a BEST behaved mind.

Very complicated (tai fuza)

The negotiations were tai fuza, the job is tai fuza, the paperwork's tai fuza. A fantastic phrase to express that something is a pain. The "very" in tai fuza can also mean "too much", it really depends. Keeping those blurred lines in mind, tai fuza is more an exclamation than an argument. It conveys more an emotion than actual information. On a scale of BEST behavior, it reveals a lot of temper. It's more than just the usual tip of the iceberg, unless the person is absolutely enraged.

Tai fuza is a common first refusal, an utterance that doesn't aim to overthrow the plan. The player of this card doesn't thirst for attention. Likewise, the person can't expect a big response. As a leader you can decide what's best for the team: discuss every input or brush over the complaint and go for the plan? Sometimes, tai fuza is merely a grumpy remark on Monday mornings.

Not convenient (bu fang bian)

Bu fang bian has nothing to do with convenience, but all to do with convincing. It's the magic bluff of fantasy language. A tea shop assistant might tell you that buying this brand is really not convenient. Actually, she would love to sell you a pricier brand! Wouldn't that be a lot more convenient?

In a literal sense, bu fang bian can also mean "not comfortable". When a post office clerk tells you that the option you chose is not comfortable, he doesn't really emphasise the tragic fate of your parcel in a lousy dark corner during freight. To him, the plush airmail DX just seems a lot more convenient.

Sure, not every shop assistant or post office clerk will bluff. Some may use the same expression, but not as a businessman- or woman. As a caring citizen they worry about the glory of China. What a national loss of face if a foreign guest has to wait for six weeks until a parcel arrives! Chinese patriots and bluffing model clerks, each of them is BEST by definition.

(RIKSHA DRIVER:) JUST AROUND THE CORNER?

BU FANG BIAN!

Here you go: Two examples and we're deep inside fantasy talk. It seems we're already investing too much thought in the simplest of words. What on earth could they possibly mean? Decoding is part of the magic. Fantasy talk is a two-way road. It's implication as much as interpretation. It's writing and reading, it sparkles from within and reflects the glitter all around. I admit, being on a sparkle vision all day can give you a headache. To warn you from the dangers of over-translation, here's the story of the wedding couple's gift.

The story of the wedding couple's gift

You're cursing those overboard wedding preparations? Then you haven't had a Chinese wedding debriefing! Wedding couples are given, among other things, money from relatives and friends. There can be fantasy talk implied in the money that is given, especially if the giver acts within a family network. In other words: always.

Our couple-of-exemplum celebrates their wedding and receives a number of envelopes with cash. After the wedding, they calculate and tally the earnings. The bride's aunt & uncle gave what the couple calls a "petty sum". They compare it to the

amounts that were given on other nieces'
weddings. The bride's sisters and cousins all got a
thousand Yuan more.

"What is that supposed to mean?"

"Are they mad at us?"

"Did we miss something?"

The couple takes on a journey to solve a riddle they
don't understand. They dig out old text messages,
chat-histories and make a list of all the food they
ever catered on a dinner with the aunt. They label
every meal with their elements and Yin & Yang
qualities.

"Did we ignore her blood pressure?"

"Did we offend her special taste?"

And so on. Deng deng deng.

Eventually, they go in circles of meta-talk on
fantasy talk. From there, the riddle haunts them for
months... The story teaches us the burden that
comes with a spot on the map. And warns us not to
over-do the fantasy talk. Though sometimes, we
simply can't help it.

Can't help it (mei banfa)

That's an oldie. Until the 1980s, the economy and the market were bare of internal drive. Shop assistants were paid no matter if they sold. Their service-slogan was "Mei ban fa!". You want to leave your money at this place? Can't help it, I'm sorry.

Let's say you were asking for a teapot set for a couple of reasons: First, because you needed one, second because you wanted one, and third, because there was one, sitting on the shelf right behind the counter. The clerk would go "mei ban fa" and give it a shrug. Back to his reading, which you were bold enough to interrupt. You would insist and point to the teapot set, you would even make the clerk turn his head and actually face the goddam thing. But still, all you would get was a mei ban fa.

Mei ban fa didn't stand for anything in particular. It didn't go against bossy customers or underpriced products. Maybe it owed to the kafkaesque nature of business in a planned economy, but who knows. What we know is that our pre-1980s shop assistants had no incentive to assist the shoppers.

Today, with all the biz and buzz in China, clerks are more likely to pounce at you. They use fantasy talk to tickle your urge to splurge. The only ones who are retro enough to give a straight-face refusal are city office workers and work unit secretaries. In their dialect of Fantasy Hua, they might tell you they "don't know" (bu zhi dao). It's not against you. You know that they know. But more importantly, you should know that you don't know... right?

Number 6: I know that I don't know

This quote by ancient Greek philosopher Socrates gives us a good compass for our never-ending maze. Just as the China labyrinth is meant to grow, become more complicated, challenging and surprising, so are we. At a certain point we'll see that there are no certainties when it comes to Chinese BEST behavior. Even if I call myself a China expert, I always keep in mind that there are things I don't know.

The only thing I can do is to grow familiar with China's unpredictability. From that moment on it's all about social negotiation. And society, that's all of us!

My debatable suggestion: Why not give our Socrates a cocky little twist:

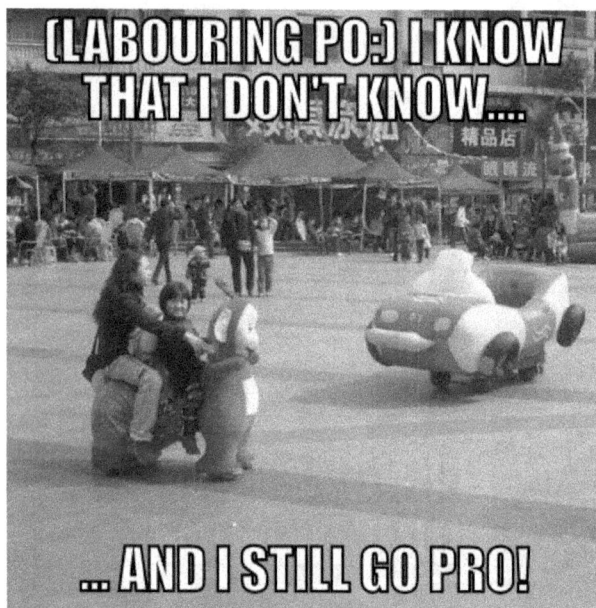

(LABOURING PO:) I KNOW THAT I DON'T KNOW....
... AND I STILL GO PRO!

Maybe that's a bit too over-confident, but it's a remedy for those who don't see the social negotiation. Those who go like:

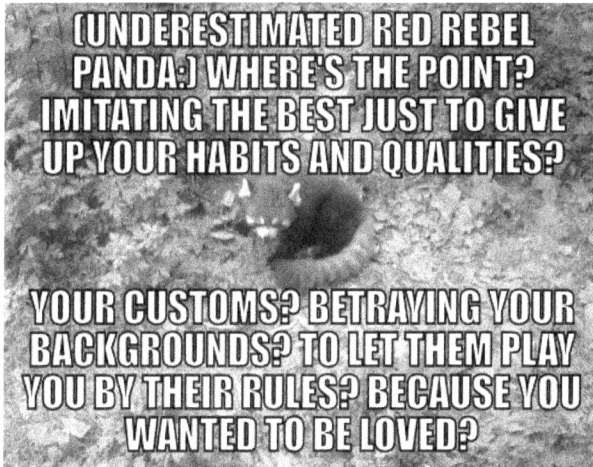

(UNDERESTIMATED RED REBEL PANDA:) WHERE'S THE POINT? IMITATING THE BEST JUST TO GIVE UP YOUR HABITS AND QUALITIES?

YOUR CUSTOMS? BETRAYING YOUR BACKGROUNDS? TO LET THEM PLAY YOU BY THEIR RULES? BECAUSE YOU WANTED TO BE LOVED?

These questions were raised by my veteran China friends, notably guys who had more than enjoyed the Middle Kingdom. They had avoided foreigners except one another - all for the benefit of integration. The same-sex-but-different-cultures couple wouldn't miss a chance to assimilate to Chinese BEST behaviour. "In return", as they put it, their Chinese network accepted them when they came out as lovers. Leaving the dubious equation aside, I think they knew why they valued cultural immersion. Growing as a couple had long been their inter-cultural trump. So how on earth did they end up all dramatic about "giving up one's culture" and "playing by their rules"?

The couple who got drunk

My friends were sparkling all over the place (and I don't say this as a cliché pun). They became active members of a local community, came out without causing an earthquake and kept on fostering ties. However, they somehow forgot how to use the word "No". Sure, yeasaying brought them further in their China ambitions, but it also created a fatal dynamic.

Originally, they'd come on good premises:

The Mediterranean friend chanted "Just go with the flow, open your arms, wide and free. Let it all rush in. Breathe it, all, and celebrate and taste it!"

His Dutch partner stated: "Absorb."

Their mix of good intentions would work. They got more entrenched in the social network, never forgot to return a favour and even kept a record of the transfer of presents. Actually, that last bit should have made them re-assess their so-called "progress"... but the flow of events felt like total integration.
Things had already gotten out of hand and the couple didn't notice. It was one night when friends

and their connex had brought them to a restaurant to have dinner in a private compartment. That was when the flow became a torrent.

Rice wine made an early first appearance that night. Soon, the liquid became the centre of social interaction. The host was the first to make a toast with them. The rest of the crowd followed suit, circling the table, proposing a toast to every guest. Then our foreign friends were asked to do the same: going "cheers!" in tours, once, twice, and so on. Each clink was followed by a bow and a smile and people would urge them to toss off the shot.

In a stealth manner – like Peter Parker switching to Spiderman – the night became a teenage party, except that our friends' friends were government officials. The foreigners were the middle school geeks who had long been seeking to chill out with the cool kids. Crumbling beneath the weight of peer pressure, the geeky kids were soon to cross their uncorrupted drinking limits...

(TERRACOTTA WISDOM:)

BEING PART OF THE COOL KIDS FEELS GREAT ...UNTIL IT DOESN'T. LET ME TELL YOU THAT!

The Dutch had to throw up in the bathroom adjacent to the private compartment. The Catalan went home and to bed with the booze in his system. He woke up with a throbbing two-day long headache. Hangover custody had him pondering: "How did we get there?" By contrast, the spewing Dutchman reported a genuine sensation of "loosing face" for that he had failed to hold the liquor and food. He was sure to have offended their host. Unlike his partner, he didn't get to question their China-mode. Instead, he reflected in a BEST Chinese manner.

Eventually, the pondering one asserted to be sober – both from the booze and China. He put it all on the table, his qualms about total immersion, cultural exchange, assimilation and integration. Sparking a great discussion, which turned into a conflict about good and bad expatriates. When they approached me with their views and asked for my useful advice, I gave them pro-mode.

Pro-mode

Pro-mode doesn't officially break with Chinese etiquette. As a pro you subvert it like a secret agent, while cashing in the credit for BEST interaction. It gives you control over your deeds and un-blurs the dynamic, based on good knowledge of Chinese etiquette and the common agenda (e.g. what is usually due on a Chinese rice wine night). Even outside the rice wine scenario, pro-mode can help you to be more active than passive. On the cockiness spectrum, it places you closer to the assertive side.

Yes, there's a reason I call it pro, and yes, it's not for the rookie. You're a pro once you know how you resonate. The many encounters with Chinese people have helped you to reflect some home-grown habits. You might have discarded a few and kept others by will.

In pro-talk you can balance between your own uninhibited tongue and the fantasy language you've learned. Agenda-wise, your experience tells you what's next. At the same time, you know *that you don't know*. You're alert for the unforeseen. You can spot it before it hits you in the face and sometimes even react in time.

This is the gist of pro-mode. It's applicable to every occasion, be it teamwork in science, political talks or business negotiations.

Well, before you get too excited, let me explain to you how pro-mode feels. In pro-mode you feel awake and in step with the flow. You're present. Just like non-stop sparkle vision, being self-conscious and attentive can be draining, but at the same time even the BEST of China will not overwhelm you anymore.

Let's tend back to our foreign friends and their drinking culture problem. On a business dinner they can gratefully accept the first drink and still go pro. Sure, going for the first will kick off the litany. The domino of rounds and one-on-one toasts, including the host's obligation to re-fill. The sooner they dry, the sooner the refill arrives. This is where the pro comes into play: sipping as little as possible, sometimes barely wetting their lips. Covering the mouth while they're drinking, not just for the sake of the phony, but because the ancient Chinese used to do the same. Song Dynasty gentle restraint? Absolutely pro!

*** OBJECTION ALERT***

Does the "trick" pull your face in a frown? Do you feel weary about the bluff?

Then Pro-mode 2 will quell your protest.

Pro-mode 2

If Pro-mode 1 is "pro" as in professional, then Pro-mode 2 is "pro" as in proactive. The one in charge is you, not your drinkmates. And yes, you're still good mates all the while. This advanced pattern won't leave them any room to steer you. Instead of merely reacting to their courtesies, try to be courteous yourself. Approach them and simply speak a toast. This will put them in a reacting position. They will focus their attention on how to answer your friendly invitation. No more making sure that you drink. Your bluff won't be noticed. Your act will be yours. You won't be a guest and they won't be your host. You've taken their sceptre!

(BAMBOO ORGY PANDAS:)

IT'S GOOD FOR YOUR BRAIN!

Sunds good? Then here's another one: Imagine someone putting a pig's brain on your plate, urging you to eat.

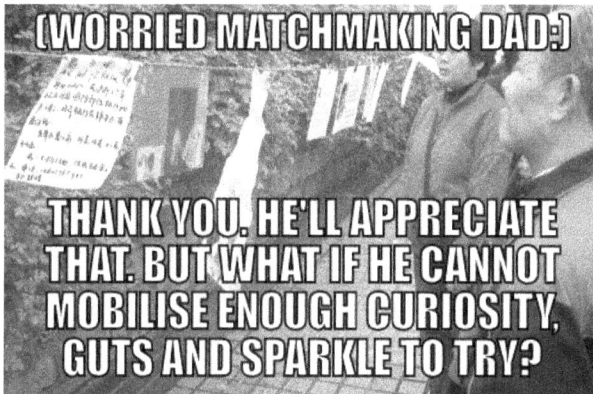
(WORRIED MATCHMAKING DAD:)

THANK YOU. HE'LL APPRECIATE THAT. BUT WHAT IF HE CANNOT MOBILISE ENOUGH CURIOSITY, GUTS AND SPARKLE TO TRY?

So how would you deal with the gift? - My useful advice: rule the moment. Pick up a random topic to divert the attention from your plate. You can even flip the brain around as you're speaking, just to indicate some minimal interest. Later, when they ask you how it tasted, you can say it was good. Since the brain still occupies your plate, they'll read it as "Thank you, I'm full." No refill. No pressure. No shame.

Pro-mode allows you to go with the flow without getting swept away. It makes you feel less hosted, more active and capable to cope with the BEST to come. Just experiment with it and don't forget to have fun!

We're up for the final bend on our circuit of manners. As we all know from our childhood, the final number connects to the first. With Socrates at hand, we don't even need to bend it too hard to return to Confucius. We're that familiar with quotes like "I know that I don't know", we're almost inclined to post them on our blog.

The slogan is easily turned into attitude. Attitude needs practice and soon it translates into manners. We can easily exploit the aphorism and produce a manual of seemingly useful advice, but can we also go the other way round? Can we trace the slogan in the act? Can we deduct the idea from the sparkle we observe?

5 (五)

6 (六)

7 (七)

I imagine something like a sparkle-tracker or Confucius-detector that marks the magic in the air. You could simply film a scene and identify the source of the sparkle. You could record a conversation with lots of fantasy talk, a filter would dissect the echo of a guy who was born 551 BC. An alarm could indicate that someone is acting at their BEST. No more fuss with fuzziness - clarity!

<u>Number 7: the sparkle-tracker app</u>

If I was the one who developed such an app, I would hold it back like the code for a new type of bomb. Dropping this monster would surely make the Internet collapse. China's culturecrazy public would bask in the joy of tagging their roots, crowning the most authentic members of society and unmasking the ones who subvert it with unsparkling Westernness.

The culturenatic nation would love to make each other face the logo and the lense of their phones. The victims would yodel "Eggplant!" (the Chinese equivalent of "Cheese!")

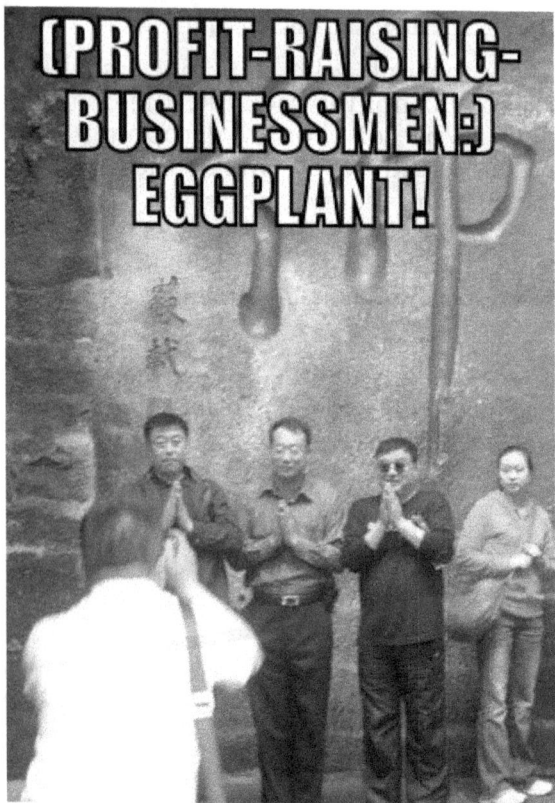

(PROFIT-RAISING-
BUSINESSMEN:)
EGGPLANT!

...thinking they are photographed. On a Beijing metro train, people would hold their phone in a vertical position, pretending to write a text, while scanning the stranger who's sitting across. Rome's Colosseo would curl a sulky lip in neglect, knowing that the tourists don't take photos of the building but of other Chinese.

When someone values the collective, radars would ring an alarm louder than anything that has ever come off a Chinese phone (and that's a lot, let me tell you that!). A new genre of selfies would be born – auto-analysis. Flexing their intercultural muscles, the most obsessed selfie-takers wouldn't wanna glisten like bodybuilders do – they'd labour to sparkle. Finally, intercultural trainers could deliver some scientific feedback, helping to set their participants straight. Mark Zuckerberg would show off his sculpted intercultural persona on TV. Soon, there'd be genetically modified babies, so that our desired offspring holds the mental DNA of their future business partners. People would make their cloud burst with photo galleries, saving their personal "BEST of Conduct". The app could classify your every act and motive. If you held back your temper, ego or pride, it will tell you why.

"That's when you didn't go first to fetch the food from the middle of the table. Look how you sparkle next to cousin Zhou!"

"Kudos. That's when you stopped an awkward silence to keep the lively atmosphere running. The chatter wrapped us in a warm embrace."

"That's when you used both hands to hand over a fifty Kuai bank note even though your right elbow was itching like hell."

Deng deng deng. There could be countless examples. The Confucius-tracker movement would become the biggest mass movement in Chinese history, fueled by the people's frenzy for morals, traditions and mentalities.

Leaving our concern for the Internet's capacities aside, there are some ups and downs to releasing this killer-application. As a benefit, we could understand the dynamic of mental DNA. We'd actually *see* that ancient philosophy is not a stage setting, posted up in the background of the Chinese play. In fact, it's the buzzing magic in the air, when someone is again on their BEST behaviour. The app would have a huge spin on society, highlighting the vividness of Chinese discourse. Even those of us who don't speak Chinese and follow Chinese media would know: The Chinese people love to debate their Chineseness.

At the same time, the app would be like Cillit Bang to our dear cultural germs. Social negotiation would be a thing of the past. China's mental DNA would be an open book to any citizen and visitor alike. Knowledge would overpower curiosity. Smartphones would kill our discourse.

(CULTURE COWBOY:) YEAH SURE... *CHUCKLES*

BUT IS THAT WHAT WE WANT?

Exactly, we LOVE social negotiation, and therefore...

Keep playing!

Chinese etiquette is a never-ending maze, intercultural exchange a game without limit. Keep playing this game. You don't have to harvest knowledge to learn. You don't have to wear a librarian's thick frame of glasses to see the backgrounds. The Chinese people will bring these backgrounds from the shadow to the spotlight. Let them play. Play along. Toss those apps. Engage with your roots, customs and manners on a personal level and you'll become part of the bigger discourse.

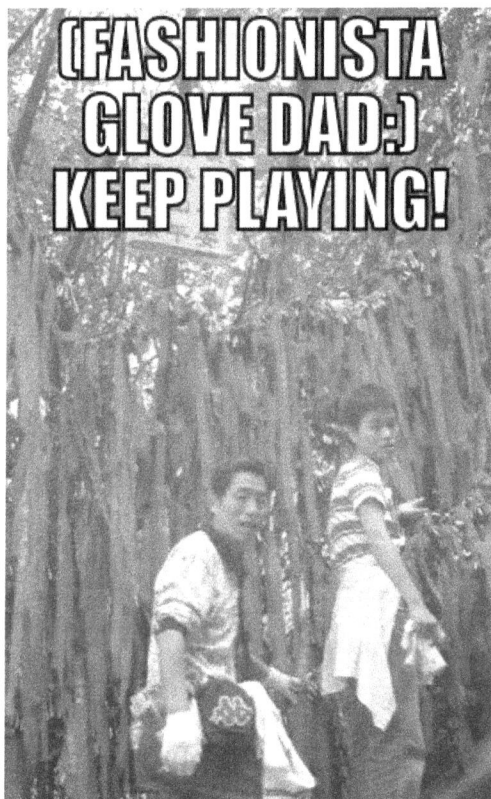

(FASHIONISTA
GLOVE DAD:)
KEEP PLAYING!

Conclusion: China-by-numbers

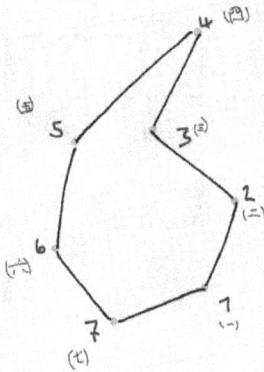

Our China-by-numbers. Doesn't it look like....
eeehm, well... if you turn it that way – no, hang on
– this way.... actually, turn it... isn't it... ?

Well, not much of a picture I guess. The drawing-
by-numbers could be anything, right? And nothing.
Nothing but straight lines and corners, the last one
leading to the first. Like we're going circles in a

maze. You've followed the advice, barely developed some orientation, nurtured you inner compass with what you call experience, and there it is again – that damn first corridor we've crossed a million times.

Closing our circle, I release you to your next intercultural project, your business trip or political tour. Our China-by-numbers is only a sketch of an intercultural approach – employ it at your will. China is an engaging topic and I know you'll add your numbers. You will tweak out the details you care about the most. Get China into shape. Sculpt it, trim it, paint it. Afterwards, I recommend you to destruct. Recklessly! Mercilessly! Painfully!

Shatter those cornerstones, smash the compass and burn your remaining meat and potatoes. For this, I'm offering CHINA MOST MISBEHAVED COUNTRY. It's a comedy complement to the journey we've shared. In any case, don't forget to leave a review and spread the word. I'm grateful to anyone who supports me in my writing about China, whatever that is…

Jiu Ling

"50 Shades..."-extra chapter: Solaris

For the grand final, we have to find a nickname for our favourite and most cherished China. Now that we're on first name terms, what is it that China IS? To nick you a name, I'm dishing up an ultimate metaphor, which is a bundle-exclusive.

After all my antics with germs and spiders and a mental DNA, it's clear I'm sticking to the sciences theme. Why not let China be a planet? A planet can signify a biosphere, it's full of life and deserves to be conserved. We're well advised to respect its nature and treasure its goods. And yet it evolves and it can't be tamed. If we think of a planet in space, we imagine the mysterious places we still haven't ticked off our list. Planets invite us to dream and to speculate. A planet is a part of the all-encompassing whole, the universe.

(POINTING-FINGERS-AT-PEOPLE-LESS-DRUNK-THAN-HIM DUDE:)
ORGANIC? COMPLEX? STRANGE AND INTERTWINED? LET CHINA BE A PLANET!

With this mission brief at hand, I went spacing around in my head. As it proved unfruitful, I continued the quest in my library. I came across a book by Stanislaw Lem, "Solaris". The eponymous planet is sort of an actor in the story, but all we learn about it comes from a nerd. Dr. Kris Kelvin studies the planet from a research station that hovers near the surface of Solaris. Kelvin's mind is tripping. In the beginning, it seems he only struggles with the solitude aboard. As he delves deeper into the mysteries of the planet, his condition gets worse. Is it Kelvin's mind or Solaris? Who or what plays the wicked magic on him? Can Kelvin escape the spell?

The author Lem explores even more questions, but we should be good with this China mold. The researcher-planet relationship is full of mystery and darkness. For our China-nickname, let's leave out the dark and only take the sparkle. Let's call it the friendly little brother of Solaris!

(AWKWARDLY BLUNT
APARTMENT-SPIDER:)

ALTHOUGH, I COULD EASILY
TRANSFER THE IMAGE OF A
SCHOLAR-GONE-CRAZY TO ONE
OR THE OTHER SINOLOGY
DEPARTMENT... BUT ACTUALLY, I
BETTER NOT SAY THAT... RIGHT?

Special Dedication

To the world's tenderest Wall-E, who has a laser-sharp vision for spelling mistakes.

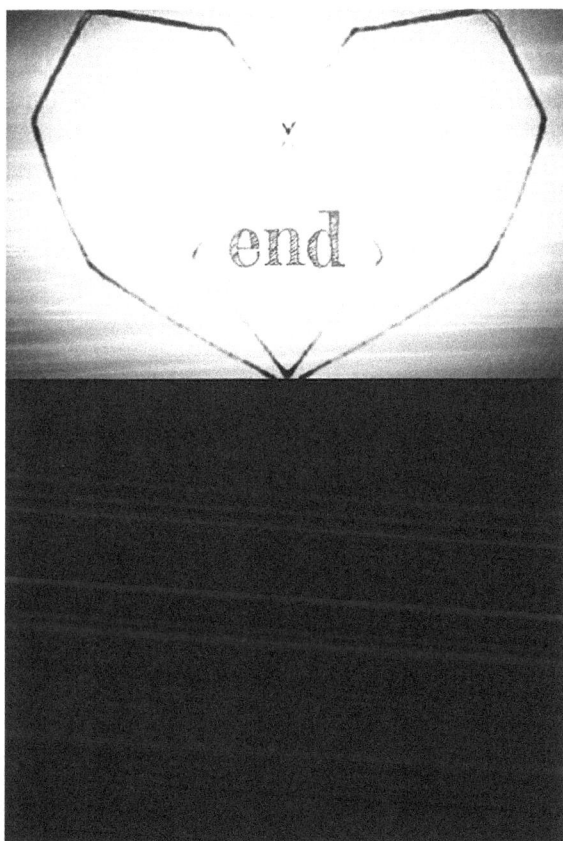
end

Prepilogue

More or less everything I wrote in Book 1 will be subject to massive destruction in Book 2.

Prologue

CULTURESHOCKING NEWS - Feb 16, 2027 - CHINA MOST MISBEHAVED COUNTRY

On Feb 16, 2027, a newspaper reveals the most misbehaved country: China. The Chinese people rock'n'roll, breaking all the rules, especially their own.

2027 is a long time to go. Until then, this guide will put you on your bestest behavior. Get your dos and donts while they're useful, learn about manners and customs as long as they're fresh. Lay back, and feast as these visuals guide you through 69 new and exciting lessons on Chinese etiquette. CHINA MOST MISBEHAVED COUNTRY takes on a wrecking ball stance to cultural guiding.

It's full of humour, pace, colours and pop. Get your daily fix, reading it chapter-by-chapter, or take that overdose you need in times of culture shock, China blues or chinostalgia. Suitable for newbies and veterans alike, in preparation for a trip as well as to debrief, this one is a must.

Content: #Business, #Culture, #Food, #Travel, #Leisure and #Friendship - in random succession.

Jiu Ling's CHINA MOST MISBEHAVED
COUNTRY

Dedication

To Abir, Adrian, Aicha, Amal, Amira,
Andrea, Anita, Annet, Annette, Cedric,
Charles, Christin, Christoph, Civan,
Danhui, Dunja, Elif, Fan One, Fan Two,
Francesco, Hamza, Han, Heidi, Huang
Yan, Iris, Iroda, Jakob, Jasmine, Javier, Jib,
Jie, Julia, Kareem, Laura, Lena One, Lena
Two, Lisa One, Lisa Two, Lucas, Maha,
Maja, Makieu, Marie, Merve, Nadia,
Nadine One, Nadine Two, Naoual,
Niccolai, Nihad, Nora, Nur, Nurcan, Onur,
Othman, Paul, Philip, Ramon, Rania,
Sarah, Sissi, Sophie One, Sophie Two,
Sophie wie Coffee, Stasa, Tina, Tom,
Victoria, Yolanda, Yulia, Zouhair and the
one who didn't come.

A guide in 69 chapters

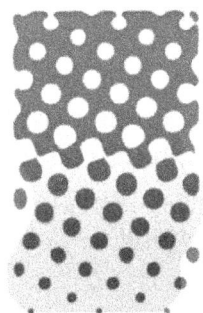

50-70%

In China, they make you do these… things. They make you drink rice wine, a liquor of fifty to seventy percent. The better the product, the better the taste. However, even the best brand of rice wine will taste like nothing but a liquor of fifty to seventy percent. Although they know that, they make you do these things. It's a custom. #rice wine #customs

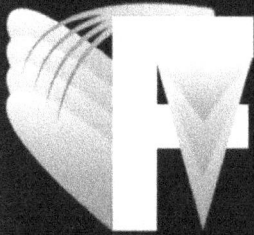

FRUITS ARE
INNOCUOUS

The choice, the wrapping as well as the giving and accepting of gifts should be handled with care. Let's talk about the gift. Fruits are innocuous, but only in even numbers, with a few exceptions: Durians, also known as the smelly fruit, are an olfactory offence. Any kind of fruit in a quantity of four is evil, despite the even number. Eight is very good, so let the fruit be small. A friend of mine brought his host family eight gigantic watermelons from Xinjiang. Because he was generous, he gave them the bus as an extra. Now that the family accepted a bus full of fruit, they felt very ashamed. Usually, families will try to refuse what you give them. This prevents them from shame. #fruits #gift #shame

S

STORMING INTO AN
OFFICE OCCUPIED BY
A LANDLORD, AN
EMPLOYER OR A
NIGHT CLUB
MANAGER

In many expat working contexts, there will be someone whose job it is to care about you. You would do well to never leave this person again. The person will prove the most valuable, irreplaceable and caring in times of severe crisis, particularly moments in which you would otherwise find yourself storming into an office occupied by a landlord, an employer or a night club manager, screaming unharmonious things. You won't have to do that, it would make the world fall apart anyway. There will be the buddy who is paid to take care of you lots. He or she can act as a mediator, which is always the best thing to do, especially since you're a foreigner. #the buddy #harmonious

BUSINESS TRIP

The choice, the wrapping as well as the giving and accepting of gifts should be handled with care. If you visit China on a business trip, bring presents as well. If your company doesn't do merchandise, try to get a tangible give-away product at the next best business occasion, e.g. a conference or fair. These mascots and penholders somehow tell a thing about your work. #gift #business

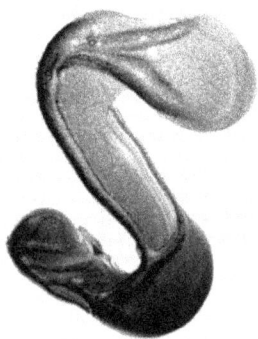

SHAME IS A
SURTAX

Bookkeeping #theChineseway: It's the first fiscal end of the year for your brand new start-up. You decide to do the profit-loss statement twice since this is the very first time. You will have a go at the numbers, and then your Chinese partner. You review the profits and losses. In sum, it was a very good year. Even post-taxes, things look just fine. But this is only the surface. You forgot to include the very beginnings, when your company hadn't even existed. The initial talks with your partner were rough. And this is what their bookkeeping looks like: On a Chinese profit-loss statement, shame is a surtax that is taken into account, implicitly. There's no worth in reaching an agreement if one side of the deal has to go on their knees for that. #shame #business

M

MY ANACONDA
DON'T

It's not a shame if you don't drink rice wine. You may have your reasons, but tread carefully in sharing them. Now that you know, you may as well map out a strategy to avoid the chance of blunder. #rice wine #the chance of blunder #now that you know

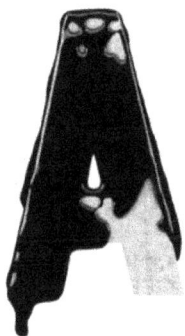

a stain on your
white flag

In China, you can get what you want, but not
what you crave. You want the chocolate? Don't
get greedy about the chocolate. It's the same with
peace. If you're in a conflict, don't stress the
issue. There will be peace, but give it some
time. Harmony is a communal achievement.
Therefore, it's even more Chinese to settle a fight
through a mediator. I admit, compared to a one-
on-one, the mediator way is a little complicated.
And this, precisely, is the value of it. If you aim
straight and force a confrontation, it
communicates greed and pushes the chances of
shame and blunder. Even if you come to peace,
there will be a stain on your white flag. #general
restraint #chocolate #the chance of blunder
#harmonious

THEY THOUGHT I WANTED
TO FLIRT WITH THEM.

The choice, the wrapping as well as the giving and accepting of gifts should be handled with care. If you plan to travel, bring presents as well. Some of your travel companions will invite you to their homes. They will be the perfect host, you can be sure about that. Try to be the perfect guest. Don't give them the box of moon cakes you were given last autumn by your Chinese employer. Give them something from your #own culture ! This brings us back to the time BC, before China. Let me share this story with you. When I was young and innocent, so to speak my own Hannah Montana, I didn't know a thing about China. In the advent of my first trip to the country, someone told me to pack a battery of deodorant spray, because they wouldn't do hygiene #overthere. I entered Middle Kingdom, equipped to turn China into the changing room of my big brother's favourite gym. On my first night in Beijing, I collapsed due to culture shock and barely made it to Walmart, where I cured myself with Pizza that had banana and mayonnaise on top. I also found out that they do deo, indeed. It took me a few months to get over this and speak to the locals. Once I started to be friendly, I saw things in a different light. I cracked their codes, read between the lines and found meaning in everything. People started to invite me to their homes. I brought them deodorant spray as a gift. They thought I wanted to flirt with them. #Miley Cyrus #gift #fruits #cake #deodorant #gym

things are dancing in your
head

On a night out, nothing just happens by coincidence. If you pay attention, you will recognise the script and learn to act according to the #rules. I know it can be hard at first, but soon you will appreciate the liturgical flow of events, emotions and gestures. First there is refusal. People refuse to sit down. There is the awkward gesture of an arm towards an arch of empty seats. No one accepts being placed on a prime spot close to the host. Everyone hesitates, but in the end they're all fine and also ashamed. They laugh and help each other with some tea. There is nervous chatter. Anticipation grows, the door opens, the waitress walks in, pushing a silver cart that is loaded with plates. There is the smell of dishes, a sweet and savoury sensation that can lure you to the worst of your behaviour. Fragrance enraptures your system, things are dancing in your head. In this very urgent moment, you can do nothing but stare at the middle of this big, round table. Shall I be the greedy one who makes the first move? Of course not. Chinese food is great, but it's never worth the shame. There will be people who invite you to eat, because they feel the same way as you. They are greedy and ashamed. Plus, they care about you and put things on your plate. Is that selfless? Not entirely, since they profit from the pressure release: only once their friends are eating, they can feel free to indulge. The wait is over. You almost forgot how good Chinese food can be. It's always a delight, I give you that. If you precede it with a good deal of general restraint, it's even better. #general restraint #night out #table #tea #shame

NIGHT-TIME
HAIRDRESSERS

In restaurants, there are usually waitresses, especially in separate rooms for dinner-and-business-arrangements. There are also waiters, but not very often. Men find employment in other service industries, such as hairdressers, but more in those which are open during daytime. Furthermore, there are waitresses in karaoke places. Note that their service may differ from the one by waitresses in restaurants, but is similar to the service by night-time hairdressers. #arrangements #the waitress #hairdressers

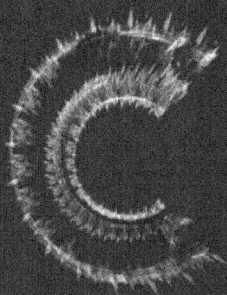

countless
explanations

Westerners are so creative when it comes to reasoning. They can come up with countless explanations for matters which simply exist to a native Chinese. For instance: Why are Chinese restaurant tables so big and so round? #tables #creative #reasoning

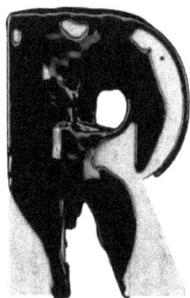

rock right up to
the side of my
mountain

The following excerpt is from a travel journal by a talented writer. She's a friend who hadn't come out to anyone but me until the moment she experienced this:

"[...] I fell into my shyness trap like I always do when a girl is hot. They both were. We exchanged hellos and started making our beds. Leaning back on the edge of my lower bunk, I was able to catch a glimpse of Tai Mountain. The window didn't offer much daylight, and still we would close the curtains to get some sleep in the hours of late afternoon. Then we would leave the hostel around midnight, share a taxi and a few words of hikemate-bonding, climb the stairs of Tai Mountain and watch the sunrise in the morning. That much I could say about me and the two Chinese girls, without even knowing their names or having attempted a hint of conversation. Silence expanded between our top and bottom bunks. Five awkward minutes later, awkward both in silence and the way I was handling those sheets, covers and cases, one of them decided to break the ice. "Which side of the mountain do you want to climb up?"

The question made me blush beneath my duvet cover, which I had thrown over my head like a ghost cape, trying to grasp the corners from inside. I fumbled for an answer, fending off a giggle that was itching my throat. Why do those Beyoncé-moments always strike me in a first conversation? There is a song about a woman's landscapes, the poor girl in the room couldn't know, and it had been roaming in my head for months. Beyoncé and her "peak, baby peak, baby peak" didn't help me at all, plus they were going to take a route called Peach Blossom Ravine, plus there were those names, you know, ...English names.

"My name is Cherry."

"And I'm Rainbow!"

That killed it! I didn't want the link from mountains to peaches to stripper names happen, I really didn't. Rainbow, Cherry and I parted ways post-taxi. I decided for the Eastern Route, had a quiet and solitary climb, save Beyoncé, who was playing in my head, on repeat. There was nothing wrong with the girls, I concluded on Tai peak (baby peak). There was something horribly wrong with me. I had to come to terms with myself, so that I would less be the kid from Grade Seven, who giggles at the mention of a three-letter-word [...]"

Coming back from Tai Shan, my friend came out to her Chinese host family, something they celebrated with lots and lots of rice wine. I was happy for her. In the following weeks, we had some good debate about Chinese English names. We agreed that names like Ruby, Candy, Foxy, Glimmer, Pippy, Pearl and Orange are funny, but feasible. At least you remember those names! We also concluded that foreigners have to choose their Chinese names wisely. No more Pi Tes and Jie Kes, please! These are names you get written on your neck in Western tattoo parlors. We decided on the following rules: 1) Your Chinese name has to relate to your own first name, but more in a subtle than obvious way. 2) It can be nonsensical, yes, but please within limits. People shouldn't think you lost a college fraternity bet. 3) It should be written with ease, in case you become famous.

Our top priority was the fame condition. We decided on numbers, because they have the fewest strokes. The result: My friend is called Liu Yi / Six-One (5 strokes) and everyone remembers her name. My name is Jiu Ling / Nine-Zero and it's the easiest name on the planet (3 strokes). Please correct me if I'm wrong about the easiest name, and if you don't have a Chinese name yet, grab a dictionary now.

Halt!

Before my most devoted readers pull their sleeves up for the needle: Don't get the Eight-Eight tattooed on your arm, even though it's the glorious eight. The pronunciation is Ba Ba and you don't introduce yourself by saying something that sounds like "Hi, I'm Daddy"... Now, last but not least: Three-Eight has a special connotation. March 8 is Women's Day, respected in China by the industry and people alike. However, somehow China ended up choosing San Ba as a very bad word, one that people use to describe a nighttime hairdresser.

#hairdressers

DEMOCRACY

Chinese restaurant tables are big and round. The reason why they are is democracy. #tables #democracy #reasoning

THE YOUNG FAT COUSIN CALLED LITTLE
SISTER GU

For the sake of democracy, Chinese restaurant tables are big and round. Each member of the dining crowd has an equal chance to start and join a group conversation. This may turn into a scene, where everybody speaks at the same time, battling for the spotlight of discussion. Imagine a whole group of cousins in their fifties, beating out their own vocal cords, trying to turn their enemies hoarse. Eventually, there's always the younger fat cousin called Little Sister Gu, the one with the volume. She's holding the attention, just to be outperformed by Big Cousin Zhao, the one with the pitch. It's a curious scene, a spotlight spin-off to Tower Defense if you will, sporting vividness and noise instead of canons and gore. While this all sounds like a whole lot of fun, some of us are neither Little Gu nor Big Cousin Zhao. If you happen to lack their vocal capacities you can always resort to a sweet tête-à-tête with your immediate neighbour. #tables #democracy #group conversations #dinner talk

PLAYING
CHESS FOR A
WHILE

· ·

Chinese business people are very generous. They bring time to negotiations. It is easier to reach a harmonious agreement if both sides have the time to play chess for a while. You guys will need the chance to calibrate your interests. Sure, this idea doesn't suit a two-day agenda. If you have no choice but force the schedule, this will be seen as a violent move. The Chinese side will showcase the Art of War. They will dodge your blow like a Tai Chi master. There will be a #smile and a cliff-hanger moment. You will leave without closing a deal. In your mind you will call it a nail in the coffin. They will call it a midway-point of good negotiations, because in case I haven't mentioned, Chinese business people are very generous: they even share their long-term perspective with you. #business #late #The Art of War

D

DID YOUR
PARENTS ALSO
WEAR DIAPERS?

The concept of privacy can be understood as a fortress in which you treasure some precious information. In the West, you don't want every colleague to enter your fortress, neither a stranger nor a travel acquaintance. In China, random co-working, strange-acting, travelling people may ask you a number of questions. How much do you earn? What do you pay for your car insurance? When will you get married? How long will the infant sleep in the same room with you and your partner? Did your parents also wear diapers when they were babies? It's like #thesepeople are plundering your fortress straight-on. You don't even have a chance to think of an eloquent answer, that is, unless you mapped out a strategy for this. #now that you know #privacy

B!

THIS IS THE CAPITAL
LETTER OF THE TEXT

READ THIS TEXT

be wise about
what you do
next

If you sit around a big, round table and happen to serve your friends tea, be wise about what you do next. Never ever let the spout of a tea pot point in the direction of a living being. He or she will turn into an open jar of honey with the bad luck swarming in like a beehive. #tables #tea #weird things

privacy

The concept of privacy can be understood as a fortress in which you treasure some precious information. Although Chinese people don't tend to rush things, they can be eager to ask you some personal questions, while having only met you half an hour ago. Don't be stingy with your gems. If you feel uncomfortable with this kind of invasion, try to wrap the private in a thick and sweet layer of cotton candy fiction. #privacy

ALL IN HD

Alright. This is going to be an awkward stunt of prose. Can you map out a strategy of coping with this? I doubt it. The following paragraph is about death. Talking about death, accidents, cancer, misfortune and failure makes Chinese people imagine spectacular things, all in HD: an open jar of honey close to a beehive. You got it? No? Then let me give you a very general example, using a #GARC, a general average random Chinese: He or she has just ear-witnessed someone else mentioning the bad. Literally, the B.A.D., as in Bankruptcy, Accident and Death. In the following, he or she sees an open jar of honey - the blundering dude - close to a myriad of bees, all of whom are actually demons outside the metaphor. They're all swarming in... #weird things #the blundering dude

SLIPPERS

Someone has invited you to their home. They will be the perfect host, you can be sure about that. You arrive at their doorstep, hand over the gift and catch a glimpse of the living room while giving that gentle handshake of yours. The whole place is sparkling clean. The family has made an obvious effort. You're wearing sneakers and for once in your life, you didn't bring your slippers. Shame on you. What do you do? You ask for slippers, but they tell you it's no problem, that their home is a mess, a dim and frigid room. Try to insist, because they do have those slippers. They're all wearing slippers themselves. This is a conspiracy. Now it's you against them. #home #gift #handshake #host #shame #the chance of blunder #conspiracies

CUTE LITTLE
FOREIGNER

Why do people make others drink rice wine? Since rice wine happens to be very strong, accepting a toast can be seen as a sign of self-abasement. This may seem true the more you observe dinners and tables and hosts and arrangements. The host can make the waitress pour a little more in your glass. Why is that? Do they force you to swallow the booze as in "Cute little foreigner, isn't he courteous!" Is it all about humiliation? The thought is, in fact, very creative, but not very useful to you as a foreign guest in China. It is also not useful to friendship. You may as well discard the thought and quit reasoning in general.
#creative #reasoning #rice wine #tables #arrangements #host #waitress #friendship #conspiracies

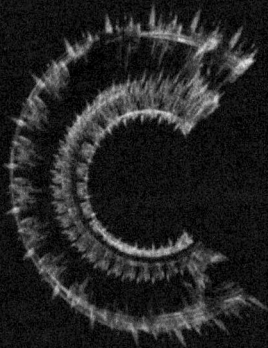

ceiling

Westerners are so creative. When they cram into an elevator, and start looking at the ceiling, are they imagining things? #creative #space

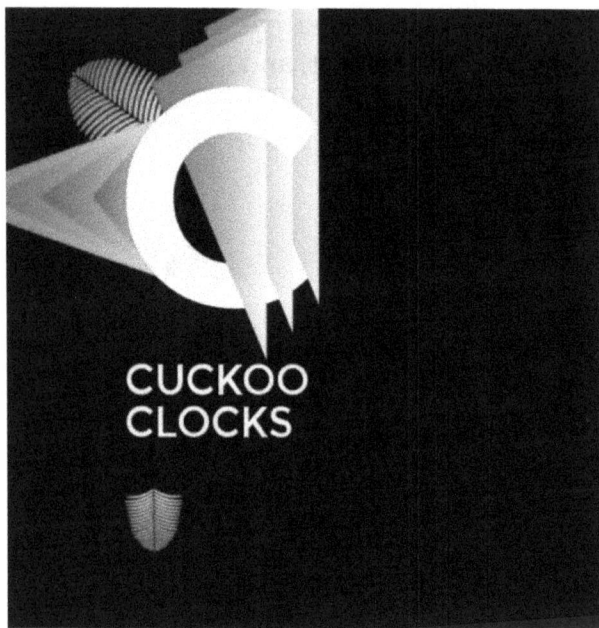

CUCKOO
CLOCKS

The choice, the wrapping as well as the giving and accepting of gifts should be handled with care. Let's talk about non-fruit gifts. Chinese people give moon cake for Moon Cake Day and a mandala of two symmetric fish to newlywed couples. They give mandalas of five bats to the elderly, even though five is an uneven number. Be careful about clocks, they point out the finiteness of life, an issue that may be avoided. Sinology hasn't settled on the matter of cuckoo clocks, though. Research on gift-giving moments is tricky, since Chinese tend to unbox their presents in private. In general, an item of local handicraft tells people a thing about the place you come from. It's very #cultural. In contrast, obnoxious city marketing tat doesn't tell a lot about the place you come from. Still, it passes. In the end it's not about the content, but about the moment of exchange. #gift #cake #the elderly #Sinology

show that you
care

Picking up someone from the airport shows that you care. Also grown-ups need to be cared for at times. #communication #grown people

poisonous spiders

A few days ago, somewhere in the West, I was sitting in the waiting room of our local dentist, when I overheard a curious thing. I learned about Miley Cyrus and, you know, #that generation. Never had I thought of a thing like a #poundandashake. That's how these youngsters call their ways of salutation. Some even graze each other's body parts as an informal greeting. Please: Don't do this in China. A gentle handshake will do. If you tend to give firm and #masculine handshakes, try to practice the virtue of general restraint. Do not pat other people's backs unless there is a poisonous spider sitting on their shoulder. If the latter applies, please be careful not to hurt the person, yourself or any living being. #Miley Cyrus #handshake #general restraint being special

On a night out, there is always a host who will make you feel like a guest. For you as a foreigner, this goes even further: Every Chinese person at the table will strive to appear like a host. They will all play their part to make you feel like a guest, because you're not only a guest on a night out, but also a guest in their country. #night out #host

TREAD
CAREFULLY

If you don't drink rice wine, tread carefully in sharing your reasons. If you follow the rule of your religion, this is a welcome fact. It is interesting, very #cultural and private, and therefore not at all considered a taboo on a Chinese dinner table. #dinner talk #rice wine #night out #privacy

F

FOR THE SAKE OF DEMOCRACY

For the sake of democracy, Chinese restaurant tables are big and round. Each member of the dining crowd has equal access to food. Everyone needs access to food, not in order to feed themselves, but in order to feed their neighbours. Things will end up on your plate. #tables #plates #democracy

terracotta warriors

I once was invited to an international business conference in China. It was on the #fourth floor of a convention centre just outside town. There were other people in the lift who were obviously invited to the same thing as me, holding that same envelope with the invitation in their hands. The doors slid closed and elevator music started to play. K-Pop, I still remember the song, that's how intense the situation must have been. Usually, people make sure that the lift is going where they want to by frantically pressing the button of their choice. But here, we were bound for the fourth floor! We became motionless like terracotta warriors, listening to K-Pop. Since I was the only foreigner, I allowed myself the blunder. I pressed four, in hopes to break the ice. Buttons were chosen, however, as my fellow terracottas were Chinese, they all chose differently:

three, five, and even #eight. The elevator zipped past the first and second floor, and we could see that the building was yet to be finished. Also the third floor revealed what looked like a Steampunk jungle of cableware. Still, there were people getting off on the third. I asked myself what kind of mischief they were having in their mind. Turned out they weren't misbehaving very much, but taking the stairs. On the fourth, where everything was finished, I met them again. Also the couple who reached us from the eighth floor. Actually, we all ended up sitting at the same table, close to the buffet. I felt really bad for going to that chocolate fondue so often that night. #4 #elevator

the big, round
table

Business talk is likely to happen - at a big and round table - in a restaurant. A party to welcome the foreigner will take place in a restaurant. A party to celebrate the ongoing stay of a foreigner will take place in a restaurant. A party to bid you farewell will take place in a restaurant. Just about every kind of party will take place in a restaurant. The party that is most likely to happen outside a restaurant is a student flat party, where everyone will strive to make things have the feel like you were just in a restaurant. #night out #business

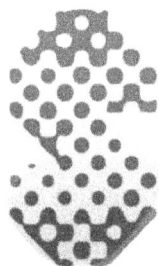

small talk and middle talk on
super scale maps

Arrangements are a very fluid concept. You close a deal, schedule an appointment for a meeting or decide on a deadline. Now there's only one way to mess things up: to consider them sealed. In order to keep the spirit from Day One alive, you'll have to check and double-check on business. Don't assume it'll be fine to call a week ahead of schedule. A week before due date, you simply cannot know how things have developed in the meanwhile. Will they be able to make it? Did they save a reminder, did they check the dropbox? What if? What if? What if? So many things can happen in China. Bearing this in mind, everybody acts like in a cheap telenovela. People make phone calls under false pretences. Never heard of those? You need a 3-step manual? Here you go: You call your friend and start the conversation as usual. This means you come up with a very random topic: food, health, gossip. This is just a starter. Don't take this talk too seriously. Post-small talk, you may move on to middle talk: There was a two-day long traffic jam on the third ring road, and I was afraid that you... (The person doesn't even live in Beijing) There's a scandal with those no-name iPhone chargers, I hope you didn't buy one... (The person doesn't have an iPhone) I've seen your town on the weather forecast and I was thinking of you (The town is a village of 5.000 and is only ever mentioned on super scale maps). To sum up: False pretences are middle talk. They show that you're not rushing the matter. They're not straight to the point, but they're getting you there. And besides, calling is caring, as my Mom keeps reminding us children. Chinawise, calling is always a very good idea, especially when you want to nurture a personal #andor business tie. Don't show that the big talk is the reason you call. Once you've gone past the middle talk, you can do the big talk: I will send you an email this afternoon with the address again so that you... Since we're planning to publish next month, I wanted to double-check... #business #arrangements #communication #tie

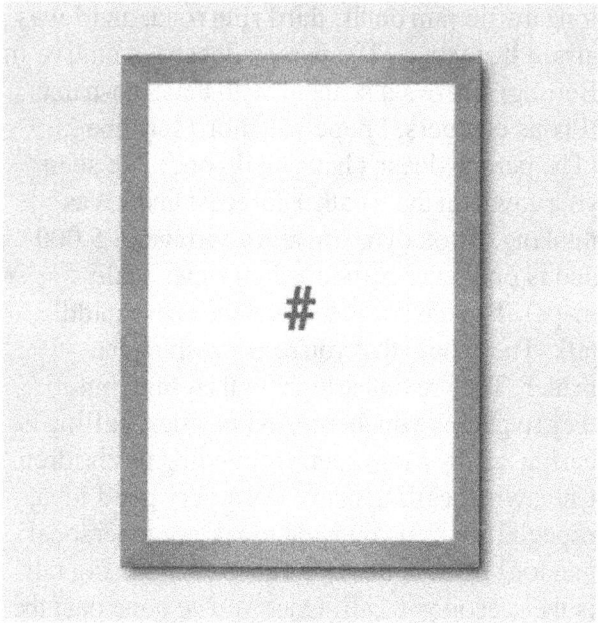

If you don't drink rice wine, tread carefully in sharing your reasons. If you abstain from alcohol, because there has been too much of it in your life or the life of your loved ones, think twice before crashing a party with a speech on the matter. During a Chinese dinner party, alcoholism is considered a heavy hashtag. In an act of harmonious wording, you may sell the reason as #familyreligion, if that is okay for you. #rice wine #heavy hashtags #harmonious

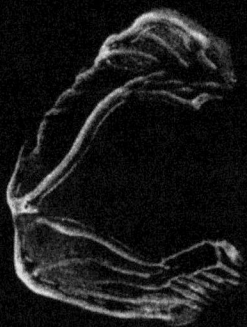

COLOURS

The choice, the wrapping as well as the giving and accepting of gifts should be handled with care. Let's talk about the wrong kind of wrapping paper. I once gave a present wrapped in shiny silver paper and people started looking at each other in a disconcerted manner. They went on saying things under their breath. They couldn't decide whether they'd seen a tiny bit more black or a tiny bit more white in this flickering silver. Irritation began to show on their faces. Their irises were ping-pong zipping left and right. Eventually, it dawned on me that both colours have a negative connotation. Black is evil and white is the funeral colour. My irises grew... #gift #black and white #irritation

This is our house
This is our rules

Dinner parties, dates, birthdays, "we're all here and love to come together"-celebrations, and not to forget: office night outings. In daily talk, all these occasions may share the same label, #party. The Chinese concept of party has little to do with a certain Miley Cyrus video, or with a Western way of party in general. Chinese get-togethers are vivid and loud. Vividness and noise are desirable. To support the happening of both, there will be food, tables and plates. #night out #tables #plates #labels #Miley Cyrus #vivid and loud

7

*things you
should put on
your to-do-list*

The choice, the wrapping as well as the giving and accepting of gifts should be handled with care. If you plan to travel, bring presents as well. Some of your travel companions will invite you to their homes. Map out a strategy before you go to China. What will you bring as a gift? Don't bring deodorant, please! Have a look at your to-do list. Does it say "stock up with deodorant" ? Delete that. Take a pencil and write down: "Stock up with light-weight souvenir tat". That will make you're your host very happy. National anniversary coins aren't bad, as long as they don't have the value of 4. #gift #money #deodorant

A THANK YOU NOTE

What Chinese people drink or eat in their lives may surprise you. Likewise, the reasons you hold for not eating or drinking these things may surprise them. Take, for instance, rice wine. There can be many reasons why people don't drink rice wine. Only a few are mentioned in this book. There may be other things that people don't consume for a manifold of reasons. The way you market them is an act of communication. Now that you know, you can map out a strategy to avoid the chance of blunder. By the way, I have a very good friend who survived China on a vegan diet, without causing too much shame. And then she proofread this guide, reducing my orthographic shame. Now can you beat that! #communication #custom #now that you know #the chance of blunder

If you don't drink rice wine, tread carefully in sharing your reasons. Don't tell people that the liquor doesn't go well with your antibiotics. You are in a restaurant with a big, round table. People take food from the middle to put it on their own and other people's plates. Instead of the latest trending flu, you may be advised to choose an innocuous medical condition. #rice wine #table #plates

/la/rly
ea/te/

It is always good to think one step ahead. This is why you're reading this book, so that you can say: Now that I know, I can map out a strategy to avoid the chance of blunder. However, when it comes to acting, try to be one step late. This goes in line with the virtue of general restraint. Slow down, hold back, watch, smile, negotiate, imitate. It's a nice little exercise. #general restraint #late #communication #now that you know #the chance of blunder

I privacy I

Group conversations are vivid and loud, hence they are desirable. They tend to be shallow and fun. However, don't think that you're safe from personal questions. #group conversations #dinner talk #privacy #vivid and loud

A

arrangements

Restaurants have separate rooms for dinner-and-business-arrangements. In the centre of the room there is a big, round table. The seat of the host is facing the entrance, preferably south. In the corner of the room, there is a waitress with bottles of rice wine and tea. Both will be served during dinner. The latter is more popular with many foreign guests. #arrangements #rice wine #tea

On a night out, there is always a host. The duties of a host include paying for the food and making everyone happy. Please note: The two objectives contradict one another. You may successfully cater a happy, noisy atmosphere, but once you ask for the bill, things fall into a turmoil. Fighting a rebellion is the final quest of a host. Without it, a host wouldn't be a host. And without a host, the guests wouldn't be guests. After all, playing the host is an honourable and popular job. Sometimes a little too popular, in fact: There are nights when you can't really tell who is playing the host. Ultimately, this will be settled through violence. Violence is likely to happen by the end of the night, when it comes to paying the food. #rebellions #host #pay the bill

PRIDE

Westerners are so creative. They can come up with endless ways of reasoning matters which simply exist to a native Chinese. For instance: Why do people make others drink rice wine? Since rice wine is very strong, it is not a shame to raise the question inside of your head. However, it is a shame to tell a Chinese that rice wine is disgusting. It is a shame to them and to you. #creative #reasoning #rice wine #toast #shame

IMAGINING THINGS

No matter where you are, what you do and who you're with, it's always good to think one step ahead, all in the sense of: Now that you know, you can map out a strategy to avoid the chance of blunder. If you don't know, then be #creative. #now that you know #the chance of blunder

HIERARCHIES

For the sake of democracy, Chinese restaurant tables are round. Despite this reasonable fact, there is quite some hierarchy at work, depending on seating arrangements. There is usually a host who will make you feel like a guest. #night out #host

PULLING A
LONESOME

No food without vividness and noise. In other words, you are expected to eat out with friends. In fairness, you can always pull a lonesome, but make sure you're going to a Chinese Muslim Noodle Place. The food there is so mouth-wateringly good, you will experience your own kind of vividness and noise - something like a Spring Festival of fireworks exploding in the gustatory system of your tongue. Also, Chinese Muslin Noodle Places are equipped for the loners and you can always recognise them. These restaurants don't have big, round tables. Their seating arrangement resembles a Chinese classroom, minus the blackboard. Instead, they all have the same oversized menu on the wall, with a green background and pictures of the meals. You've seen one, you've seen them all. #tables #solitude

DID YOU PUT
ON ENOUGH
SUNSCREEN?

Remember. You serve the others tea, because you care about them. You organise their travels, queue up for them at the station, pay for their food, carry their groceries and ask directions for them. You ask them if they've eaten enough. You ask them if they've put on enough sunscreen. You bring sweets for their child, Yin food for their Mum who has been a little too much on the Yang side lately. All this works out fine, because people care about you just as much as you care about them. #the truth

THEY FIND COMFORT IN THE
THOUGHT THAT YOU'RE DOING
THIS BECAUSE YOU'RE A
FOREIGNER.

They watch you. Closely. They watch you blowing your nose and putting the tissue back in the pocket of your jeans. They find comfort in the thought that you're doing this because you're a foreigner. Still, they taste bile watching you blowing your nose and putting the tissue back in the pocket of your jeans. #tasting bile

NO PERSONAL TIE WITHOUT A MENTION OF GRANDMOTHER'S LEFT GLASS EYE.

In the West, the concept of privacy can be understood as a fortress in which you treasure some precious information. In China, even a random travel acquaintance may want to invade your fortress of personal data. They may not hack your mobile (you know, ...#nerds rarely travel) but they will pester you with questions. Plundering each other's fortress is the bottom line of social connection. No personal tie without a mention of grandmother's left glass eye. Even if you falter in your awkward response, tell them what happened to grandmother's eye. Sharing is caring. #grandmother's left glass eye #privacy

In cheap telenovelas,
people trip on the street

In cheap telenovelas, people trip on the street and they can't get up on their own. Luckily, there will soon appear a helping hand, one that even belongs to the love of their lives. But as we all know, things are different in the real world. Speaking of the real world, can it get any realer than China? If you trip on the street in China, there are demons involved. Since demons are contagious, you will end up waiting for a generous while, in hopes that Romeo saves you. As if you and your aura were magically sealed off by invisible barrier tape. Suddenly, and for once in this country, you have a hell lot of space for yourself. No one will offer you a hand to reach out for. They do well not catching what made you trip in the first place. Those who help you are expected to meet the same fate as you. Of course, there are bigger accidents than tripping on a

pavement. The bigger the accident, the more generous the barrier tape.
#imaginary barrier tape

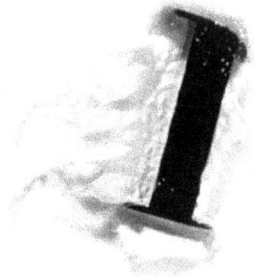

I

INCREDIBLE!

No personal tie without a mention of grandmother's left glass eye. People will pester you with personal questions to nourish their connection with you. If what they ask for is too private, there's no shame in cheating. You can invent your whole life if you want to. As long as you give, it doesn't really matter what you give. The building of personal ties is more about the moment than the content of exchange. #grandmother's left glass eye #privacy #tie

ON FEEDING

When people want to make you feel like a guest, they will probably make an effort to express that they care about you. On a night out, they can show this by fetching some food from the centre of the big, round table. The food will end up on your plate. #communication #night out #host #plates

1m²

The concept of personal space can be understood as a 1m² blanket with you in the centre. If people stand on your blanket, many things are suddenly considered indiscreet. Chewing noisily on a chewing gum, overtly looking at those who are sharing the blanket with you, allowing your stomach to rumble, and so on. If you don't believe me, go to an elevator nearby, a crowded one of course, then cram in, chew, stare and tell your stomach to rumble. Do this as long as you're outside Middle Kingdom. In China, there can be so many crowded situations that people do not care about the rumbling of their stomachs anymore. Their blankets have the size of tissues, folded, and apparently they're totally fine with that. #space

exchange

The choice, the wrapping as well as the giving and accepting of gifts should be handled with care. It's more about these rules than about the content of the gift. Let's talk about the giving and accepting of gifts. Use both your hands. Using only one hand is lazy. It sends the message that you don't really care. #gift #communication #accepting

swimming in the ocean of political
debate

For the sake of #vivid'n'loud, Chinese conversations are shallow. People do not delve the waters of deep, psychological topics. Neither do they swim in the ocean of political debate. They're afraid of drowning. Many Chinese people can't swim, especially the elder generation. #dinner talk #heavy hashtags #the elderly

*pyramids
of cake*

The choice, the wrapping as well as the giving and accepting of gifts should be handled with care. Let's talk about the right kind of wrapping paper. Good colours are gold and red. As usual, we can witness a great deal of reasoning in this. Why are gold and red so incredibly good? Students of temple and palace interior design have their own thoughts on this. But their thoughts are not very creative. It is better to create your own explanation. For instance: Have you looked at Chinese supermarkets and how they manage to play their customer's minds? It's fascinating. A month before a holiday, they put their festival presents on prominent display. Boxes of moon cake are piled in delicate pyramid shapes at the entrance of the store. If it wasn't for the colour of the boxes, you'd think it a pyramid of very sweet cake, just like any other pyramid of cake. But since they're red and golden, you know that they have to be festive, that they have to be given and accepted, on Moon Cake Day, with both of your hands. You know this even a month before the middle of September. Colour conventions prevent irritation. When you give a present wrapped in gold and red, people know that it's a present. They don't even care about what is underneath the wrapping anymore. You are thoughtful and kind, and generous, and most importantly, a very good guest. #gift #cake #irritation

so many things

∿∿∿

Someone has invited you to their home. They will be the perfect host, you can be sure about that. As a guest, there are so many things you can do wrong, so you better come prepared. #host #the chance of blunder #conspiracies

CHINESE CASUAL
CHITCHAT

Chinese casual chitchat can sometimes make you feel like you're giving away your last little gem of private information. Westerners can engage in a lot of reasoning on this. Maybe it is due to #communism that people dispossess one another as a bottom line. Only then can they start to connect. #privacy #tie #reasoning

ESTERNERS
DON'T

· ·

Westerners don't necessarily imagine things when they stare at the ceiling in a crammed elevator. It shows their discomfort with a limited space. You can also observe this behaviour on a crowded subway train, in case you haven't seen it before and have no access to crammed elevators. If you want to observe Chinese people handling the issue, you are forced to go to China. I can only hint as much as the following: If they feel comfortable staring at you from afar, they will be happy to do the same in a crammed elevator. If they only steal a curious glance on a Beijing morning metro, they won't do much more from the other end of Tiananmen Square. #space #Tiananmen

THE NORM

The choice, the wrapping as well as the giving and accepting of gifts should be handled with care. Let's talk about the right kind of wrapping paper. Good colours are gold and red. Now that you know, you can map out a strategy to do it right, but to be honest, there is no real need. People don't care if you do things #right or #wrong. They know that you're a foreigner. Actually, there is so much meta-talk about what is written in here, it makes my book really useless by the time it is February 16th, 2027. People are sensible, they reflect and re-negotiate the norm. Don't tell others that you know, but rumour has it they will even forgive you if you haven't mapped out a strategy at all. #labels #gift #black and white #the truth

memo
ries...

I used to live in a Chinese suburbia, a small town, built for the middle class of Wenzhou. There was a gym, where people dropped their gym bag in the changing room. Nothing was in line with the Feng Shui. People said "Hi" to a stranger like it was a full-fledged porn conversation. Then used locker number 4, got changed and did yoga. This place was so #Western. Everyone was fearless. I miss the spirit from those years. #4 #gym

W

**WESTERNERS
MAKING SMART WITH
THEIR WORDS AGAIN**

It's #false that Chinese people are superstitious. It's the #peoplefromtheWest who can be a little esoteric about age, thinking that ageing is bad. This is totally irrational. In China, age is like maths, you add it and add it and add it, hence it's always a plus. You've lived a life of more than sixty years? Awesome. Your neighbour tops you by a decade? Even better for her. There's no doubt that ageing is good. Don't be ashamed. People simply want to know your age. They don't care about your witty wording of things à la "I'm as young as the minute is and I'm always young at heart, but to give a number, I'm a young sixty-four". Don't be funny. Give your honest reply, get used to the question, come back to China in a year's time and you'll be happier than ever to answer the question. #the elderly

💀

GAME OF
THRONES

Chinese people respect the elderly. In a game of cards, the elderly beats almost every other member of society. When you get on a bus, however, a shambling old man might offer you his seat, provided you look foreign enough. So you do look foreign enough? Are you sure? Yes? And now you think you are the card of all cards? Well then you haven't seen a Chinese pupil getting on a bus. #the elderly

SURE NOT SMALL ENOUGH

During dinner, the host will make a toast. It doesn't have to do with humiliation. It's because he or she represents something. There will be a waitress who pours rice wine into very small glasses. She will have to serve everyone as told by the host. She will have to pour a little more in the glass of certain people. The host will decide who those people are. Because you are special, you may get a little more. You will think that the glasses aren't small enough. #host #rice wine #toast #the waitress

MY SHAME IS YOUR SHAME AND
YOUR SHAME IS MY SHAME

Now take a deep breath as if you were advertising a "Spa"-flavoured detergent. This one is on harmony. Harmony is about being at peace with yourself and your surroundings. It's a communal achievement. We're all striving for it, each of us is a part of it. I would never bring shame upon myself in front of the others. They feel ashamed watching me feeling ashamed. It's a shame for the atmosphere. There are situations, where a little shame is unavoidable. In a restaurant, for example, there's got to be someone who sits at the boo-seat of honours. We all feel ashamed to take the prime spot without inhibitions. Vanity and greed are like a fart in the elevator, they're not good for the general atmosphere. For the sake of harmony, we minimise shame. #harmonious #elevator #shame

"To panda diplomacy!
Bottoms up!"

Everyone who represents something can make a toast and make everyone drink. Each of us somehow represents something. If you can't think of a thing you represent, try to think like this: People will expect you to think of yourself as a deputy of your nation. You can make a toast to international friendship. To panda diplomacy. To culture. To honour the host, or to just about anything. You can even tell them "bottoms up!" without any obvious reason. Just don't think you can drink them under the table. Many have been wrong in this before. #rice wine #friendship #toast

"
LIKE IN A TOOTHPASTE
COMMERCIAL, BUT
WORSE
"

If you're planning to eat out alone, please go to a Chinese Muslim Noodle Place, where there are no big, round tables that are made for company. Do not go to a restaurant with big, round tables all by yourself. The Chinese people will start to reason about your solitude, and let me tell you that: They can also be very creative. Their imagination will come up with a close-up of your tongue that is hosting a colony of virus, a bit like in a toothpaste commercial, but worse. In addition to that, they will analyse your posture, the movement of your jaw, the way you hold your chopsticks. It will appear logical that you're an uneasy fellow. They will picture your hopeless attempts to get a date. They will imagine your friends when you called. How they panicked from the sound of your voice, remembering you as the gloomy with the flu. How they fumbled with the cord of the phone, searching for excuses. Oh yes. They will be very creative... #creative #reasoning #solitude #friends #tables

there are no
demons

I told you lies. There are no demons. There is no imaginary barrier tape. There are only things such as hashtags. Please investigate #NanjingVerdict and #GoodSamaritansChina to find out more on this trending topic. #imaginary barrier tape

💀

Karl May never visited the
Wild Wild West,
until he did,
and it changed his writing
completely.

"If someone refuses to drink with you, here in this country, you have the right to answer his refusal with a knife or a gun; and if you shoot the offender, no one gives a hoot or two." (quote from The Treasure of Silver Lake by Karl Friedrich May)

#rice wine #customs

69

Imagine you're the foreigner on a night out. This means that you're literally the foreigner, written in capitals, sitting with a group of Chinese around a restaurant table. Everyone except you is culturally #perfect, melts into the scene like a Qipao-waitress. She's in a corner, silently holding a teapot. Be aware that in this very precise situation, you must #NOT do the following: Take those chopsticks in front of you and stick them upside down in your bowl of rice as if they were incense in an ancestral shrine. To the Chinese, this would look entirely as if you were taking those chopsticks, sticking them upside down in a bowl of rice as if they were incense in an ancestral shrine. Seriously. #the truth

Software kudos

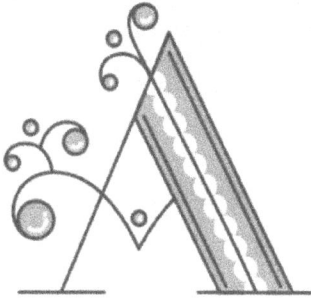

all these beautiful headings have been
made using notegraphy

Notegraphy designs by Alex Trochut,
Ariane Spanier, Atelier, Chris Rubino,
Feed, Jessica Hische, Luca Ionescu, Mario

Hugo, Mek Frinchaboy, Nathalie Koutia OFFF, Non-Format, Seb Lester, Rick Banks, Kieran Mithani, Ruiz+Company, Sara Blake, Sean Freeman, Sougwen Chung and Vruchtvlees.

Special Dedication

To Guo Laoshi, the wrecking ball.

www.ingramcontent.com/pod-product-compliance
Lightning Source LLC
Chambersburg PA
CBHW050110280326
41933CB00010B/1037